How to Design
Self-Directed and Distance Learning

How to Design
Self-Directed and Distance Learning

A Guide for Creators of Web-Based Training, Computer-Based Training, and Self-Study Materials

Nigel Harrison

McGRAW-HILL
New York   San Francisco   Washington, D.C.   Auckland   Bogotá
Caracas   Lisbon   London   Madrid   Mexico City   Milan
Montreal   New Delhi   San Juan   Singapore
Sydney   Tokyo   Toronto

Library of Congress Cataloging Number 99-67032

NOV 30 1998

McGraw-Hill

A Division of The McGraw·Hill Companies

1 2 3 4 5 6 7 8 9 0 DOC/DOC 9 0 3 2 1 0 9 8

ISBN 0-07-027100-3

The sponsoring editor for this book was Richard Narramore, the editing supervisor was Jane Palmieri, the designer was Paul Newcombe and the production supervisor was Sherri Souffrance.

It was set in Times New Roman and Helvetica by Christian Waymouth / ACT Consultants Limited.

Printed and bound by R. R. Donnelley & Sons Company.

McGraw-Hill books are available at special quantity discounts to use as premiums and sales promotions, or for use in corporate training programs. For more information, please write to the Director of Special Sales, McGraw-Hill, 11 West l9th Street, New York, NY 10011. Or contact your local bookstore.

 This book is printed on recycled, acid-free paper containing a minimum of 50% recycled de-inked fiber.

With thanks to Michael Molinaro for his support and careful editing.

Contents

Foreword

The challenge for training program designers has always been to provide clearly structured, useful, business-focused learning. For those involved in the development of self-directed learning, in whatever media, the challenge is expanded to include criteria like "engaging," "clever," "sophisticated," and "friendly."

Many designers can become so enthralled by the new technology available for the delivery of self-directed learning that they lose sight of the basic sound design principles which must apply to any media. New media will come and go *(give yourself a gold star if you resisted interactive video),* and become continually more useful as technology matures. Some of us (myself included) fully believe that Internet technology will revolutionize organizational learning systems and are making our bets that way. But whatever the media used for self-directed learning; workbooks, CBT, video, or Vulcan mind-meld, the characteristics of strong, effective design remain the same.

This workbook provides a sound, complete process for the development of self-directed learning materials which bring the focus back to the learner, not the trainer and certainly not the technology. For those who have experience designing self-directed or distance learning this book provides useful tools, examples and practices you can use right away to increase you own effectiveness. For those new to training design, this book outlines and guides you through the fundamental design process you'll want to include in every project you undertake. As training director for a global information and news organization, I've found this structure to be so vital that we "certify" all new training staff regardless of their previous experience in this methodology.

Michael Molinaro
New York City
July, 1998

Introduction

This book is divided into six modules
reflecting the six phases of the systematic approach to design

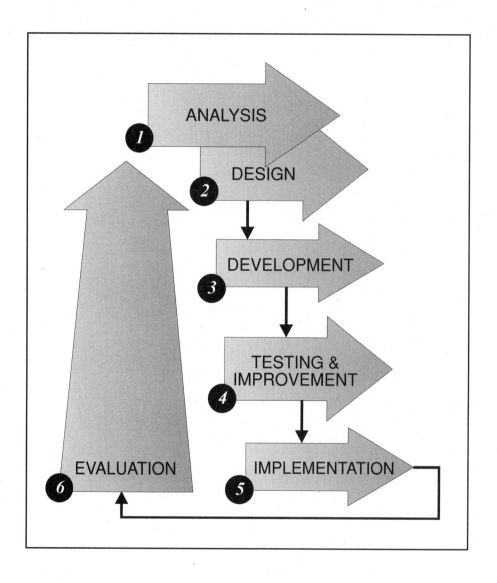

1 ANALYSIS
2 DESIGN
3 DEVELOPMENT
4 TESTING & IMPROVEMENT
5 IMPLEMENTATION
6 EVALUATION

Who is it for?

New designers of self-directed learning materials

Our target group is new training designers in organizations who want to use self-directed and distance learning to improve people's performance. This book is for you! We assume no background in instructional design.

Who else can use it?

Experienced designers

If you have some experience, take the self-assessment quiz beginning on page 8 to find the modules that are of relevance to you.

Computer-based training designers

The principles of good instructional design are the same for CBT as for any other medium. The only differences are the detailed screen design and flowcharting covered in Module 4.

Multimedia and Web-based training designers

We do not cover the features of the technology or authoring systems but this book includes the fundamentals of instructional design needed to make your multimedia solutions successful.

Trainers who design and run courses

The systematic approach to analysis and instructional design can be applied to any training method. It offers you a thorough approach to guarantee the quality and effectiveness of your training.

Training managers

The systematic approach can help you to analyze and design solutions to any performance problem. It will help you to be a better internal consultant, as well as providing a structure to manage your projects and allocate resources.

Are there any prerequisites?

Only the need to design learning materials. If you are not planning to design anything, it may be better to put the book down and pick it up again when you have a project in mind. It will mean more to you then.

You will need a project to work on for the practical exercises in Module 1.

What will it do?

'Walk through' all the stages involved in designing effective self-directed learning materials.

What will you not be able to do?

Use specific CBT authoring or multimedia tools. If you thought the book was about this, go back and get a refund.

Objective for the book

After working through the exercises using your own project, when faced with an apparent training need you will be able to start to design an effective self-directed or distance learning solution which can include:

- *text-based distance learning*
- *CBT*
- *Web-based training*
- *books*
- *workshops*
- *multimedia*
- *workbooks*
- *video*
- *audio, etc.*

What do I do next?

Do the self-assessment quiz on the next few pages to see how much you know already...

Self-assessment quiz

How to complete the self-assessment quiz

Rate how well you can answer each question

Give yourself a *2* if you can answer it fully, *1* if you think you know most of it, and *0* if you cannot answer it.

2	*Yes*	*-*	*I can answer this fully*
1	*Partially*	*-*	*I think I know most of this*
0	*No*	*-*	*I can't answer this*

Be honest!

This is for your needs only. No one else will see it.

Answer with your first response.

It will give you a good idea of the modules you can use to develop skills.

There are five sets of questions, and a *score card* on page 14.

Self-assessment quiz

Can you...	Yes 2	Partially 1	No 0
a. Describe the difference between education and training?	☐		
b. List the main reasons why people have problems with performance?	☐		
c. Describe four essential elements of a measurable objective?	☐		
d. Describe the most appropriate writing style for self-directed and distance learning?	☐		
e. Describe what is involved in the testing and improvement phase?	☐		
f. Describe a simple method for ensuring that every module in your course follows the correct design process?	☐		
g. Explain when the key activities in summative evaluation take place?	☐		

Self-assessment quiz

Can you...	Yes 2	Partially 1	No 0

Can you...

a. Name all the stages in a systematic approach to training design? ☐

b. Answer the question: 'Is training ever a solution on its own?' ☐

c. Describe the two different ways that objectives are used in self-directed and distance learning? ☐

d. Describe the key features of good page layout? ☐

e. Describe who should 'sign off' on your draft materials before they are used for testing? ☐

f. Describe the training designer's involvement in implementation? ☐

g. Name those with whom you hold summative evaluations? ☐

Self-assessment quiz

	Yes 2	Partially 1	No 0

Can you...

a. Name the focus that will ensure that training is effective?

b. Name the term used to describe the difference between what people are doing now and what you want them to be able to do?

c. Describe the two fundamental types of learning which affect your choice of method?

d. Describe the key features of good screen design?

e. Describe the format material should be in for small group testing?

f. State when you would find out about environmental factors which might hinder implementation?

g. Describe when you set up data collection for evaluation?

Self-assessment quiz

Can you...	Yes 2	Partially 1	No 0
a. Name five training methods that self-directed learning can involve?			☐
b. Describe the difference between target group and target description?			☐
c. Name the method you always consider first when choosing a medium?			☐
d. Produce a flowchart for a CBT lesson?			☐
e. State the technical name of the testing and improvement stage?			☐
f. Estimate how long a self-directed learning project will take?			☐
g. Describe why trainers often find evaluation difficult?			☐

Self-assessment quiz

Can you...	Yes 2	Partially 1	No 0

a. Describe the difference between self-directed learning and distance learning?

☐

b. Name the five criteria used to assess whether self-directed learning may be an appropriate solution?

☐

c. Describe the essential elements in structuring a unit of learning?

☐

d. Describe the common page or screen types in any self-directed learning solution?

☐

e. Estimate how long to allow for the testing and improvement stage?

☐

f. Describe all the roles to be included on a design project plan?

☐

g. Describe what you evaluate in an evaluation?

☐

Let's see how you did...

How well did you do?

Score your rating

Add up your scores and look at page 16 to see how well you did.

Question	Page						Total
	9	10	11	12	13		
a.	□	□	□	□	□	a.	□
b.	□	□	□	□	□	b.	□
c.	□	□	□	□	□	c.	□
d.	□	□	□	□	□	d.	□
e.	□	□	□	□	□	e.	□
f.	□	□	□	□	□	f.	□
g.	□	□	□	□	□	g.	□

This book is divided into six learning modules, plus an introduction.

The questions in the quiz relate to the following modules.
Transfer your total scores to here.

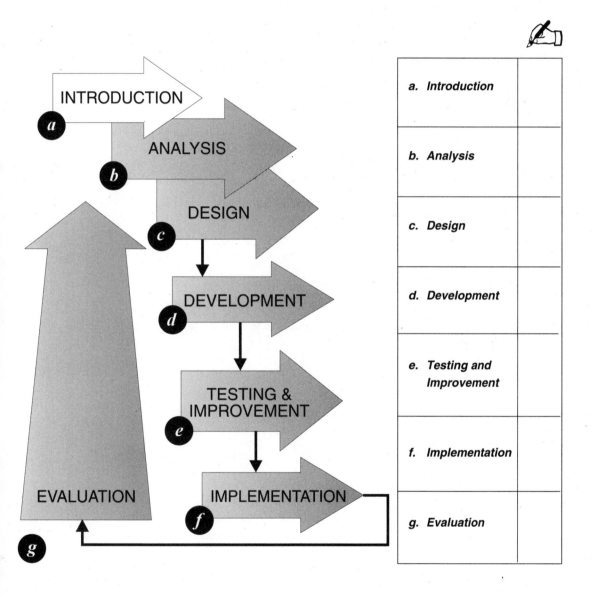

a. Introduction	
b. Analysis	
c. Design	
d. Development	
e. Testing and Improvement	
f. Implementation	
g. Evaluation	

What your score means

Score		
8 - 10	**Excellent**	You have an excellent grasp of the principles in this module and you do not need to look at it.
6 - 8	**Work needed**	Do this module and make sure you can pass the test.
0 - 6	**Start at the beginning**	Study this module thoroughly.

Use your scores to plan your learning.

If possible, discuss with your manager or a colleague how to incorporate on-the-job learning into your personal development.

Now let's check your understanding of the following terms:

- *Education*

- *Training*

- *Self-directed learning*

- *Distance learning*

What is the difference between education and training?

Write a short definition of the following:

Education is:

Training is:

Self-directed learning is:

Distance learning is:

Answers

There are no hard and fast definitions. My interpretation is:

Education is:

Imparting core skills and knowledge to be built upon.

Training is:

Skills and knowledge to raise people's performance, often organized from the trainer's perspective.

Self-directed learning is:

Individualized instruction which is available to those who need it on demand; it is:
- *designed from the point of view of the learner rather than the trainer*
- *available in short, self-instructional modules which can be studied by individuals at their own pace, place and time*
- *structured to give the learner control over his or her learning*

Self-directed learning is a general term for an approach rather than for any specific medium or method.

Distance learning is:

Self-directed learning materials that are used by learners at a distance from the center of learning.

What is the difference between education and training?

The difference between education and training is that training is about improving **performance** whereas education is about **knowledge.**

This difference is critical to the design of effective learning materials. Most senior managers hold the view that training is similar to education and that everyone is qualified to design training solutions; you just need to have an expert to present a subject to a group and tell them how to do it.

Notice that the main focus here is on knowledge and 'telling them,' rather than improving performance and learning. The power and status belong to the trainer or educator, not the learner. The application of the knowledge is left to the student to sort out on his or her own.

This 'educational' view of training still exists and you can still attend 'training courses' given by subject matter experts where the trainee is essentially passive. How many managers have you heard say, "Oh, we need some more training on X, get Sarah Smith, she knows all about it."? Little wonder that some trainers fall into the trap of the 'educational' style of training because this is what their bosses expect. To be fair to everyone involved, we can only see the world based on our own experience. Therefore, if you have only experienced formal education and classroom training, this is all you can see.

So what is training?

Training is about the **application of knowledge and skill to raise performance.**

It is not an end in itself; it only deals with 'how to' improve people's performance.

The two essential elements of training are:

- *people*
- *performance*

In simple terms, 'training' is about **helping people to do things better.**

What is learning?

Learning is what people do to develop their skills and knowledge in order to do things better.

So what is self-directed learning?

Well, the power in education belongs to the teacher:

Some traditional training retains this dynamic:

However, in self-directed learning the focus of power is shifted from the trainer to the learner (there is no trainer). Training's role is to design effective learning materials that the learner can use to improve his or her performance.

What is the difference between self-directed learning and distance learning?

For our purposes not much.

'Distance learning' is often applied to the materials and media that allow people to learn away from a source of expertice or training. It is an increasingly common delivery solution for business.

'Self-directed learning' incorporates the idea of distance learning with the notion of 'on-demand' training. Learners not only choose the time and location of their training, but can often tailor broadly developed programs to meet their specific needs. 'Self-directed learning' also often refers to performance support tools developed for learners.

Self-directed learning often involves a mix of the following media:

- books
- computer-based training
- multimedia CD-ROM
- intranet- or Internet-based delivery
- workbooks
- video, audio, etc.

We use the term loosely to mean any mix of media designed to be used by individual learners to improve their performance.

An outdated focus

Poor training and self-directed learning is often due to a focus on the needs of the ***trainer*** rather than the ***learner***. Many self-directed learning materials are nothing more than 'teaching' via another medium. To produce effective self-directed learning we need to 'get inside the shoes' of the learner and design relevant, interactive, and effective materials that he or she can use.

Trainers, leave your egos here!

You are now a learning materials designer. It is the learner who is important and your job is to help him or her to acquire the knowledge and skill needed to do things better.

The correct focus!

Remember that training only deals with 'how to' achieve something else. It is not important in its own right. What matters is **helping people to do things better**, i.e., perform better.

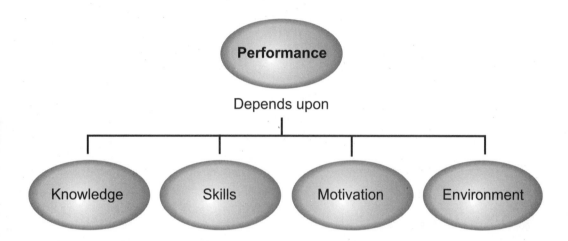

Training is only one method of helping people to acquire the knowledge and skills needed to raise performance.

It is not an end in itself

This is so important because many poor learning materials are written from the perspective of education and knowledge. The correct focus for effective materials is always to keep in mind the performance that you want to achieve and the people who are to achieve it.

Some training jargon explained

CD-ROM

Compact Disc–Read Only Memory

Multimedia

CD-ROM has allowed more than one medium to deliver on the same computer screen, e.g., computer-aided learning, video, interactive video, graphics, text, high-quality photographs plus audio.

CBT

Computer-based training, which actually has two components:
- computer-aided learning
- computer-managed learning

IBT

Intranet- or Internet-delivered learning.

Virtual reality

A combination of hardware and software for creating or accessing a computer-created environment of sound and vision.

Books

The original distance learning method!

Web-based training

Delivery of self-directed learning over a Web, which can be the Internet or an intranet.

A systematic approach

Objective

By the end of this unit you will be able to label a diagram of the
systematic approach and correctly match a set of definitions.

For many trainers, the design of training may just be a matter of selecting the right person (subject matter expert) and scheduling a number of days to run a course. For traditional courses this may be enough, as skilled presenters can adapt their material as they go along. However, for any form of self-directed learning, we need to be very systematic because the material has to be good enough to stand on its own.

A systematic approach can be applied to any training problem.

The systematic approach

This approach has six phases. Do you know any of them already?
This question is NOT a test. It is just to get you thinking!
Label the following diagram as far as you can. The answers are on page 30.

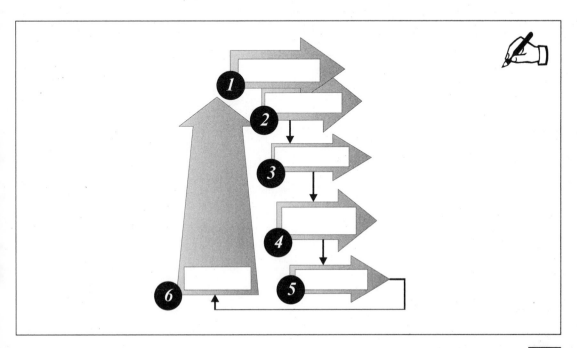

Answer

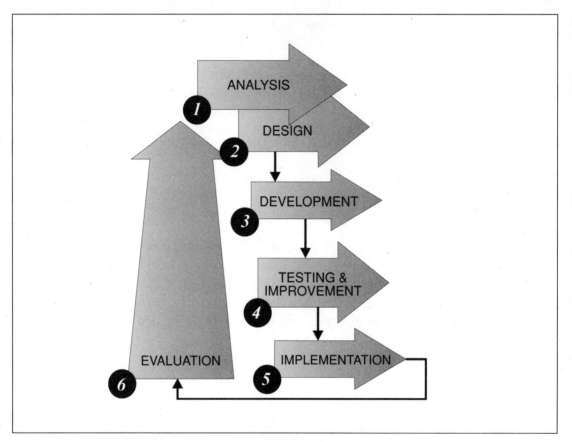

The phases in more detail

1. *Analysis*

We clarify what the performance problem is and select a number of solutions. Training is never a solution on its own. It always needs to be accompanied by some sort of organizational support and usually by information and reference material.

Once we have identified a training need, we can analyze the needs of the target group and define the final objective for the learning.

2. *Design*

We break down the topic into chunks (subordinate objectives) and then group these together into modules which can be taught together. Then we choose appropriate media and methods, and design appropriate tests and learning activities for each module.

3. *Development*

The draft material is produced, e.g., word processed, programmed, filmed, or desktop published.

4. *Testing and improvement*

The draft material is tested with representatives from the target group and progressively improved.

5. *Implementation*

The material is used by the target audience in the real environment. Designers note what extra support is needed.

6. *Evaluation*

We check the success of the solutions in solving the original performance problem, i.e., can people do what the customer wanted them to be able to do?

Quiz

Can you match the phrase with the appropriate definition?

1. **Analysis** □

2. **Design** □

3. **Development** □

4. **Testing and improvement** □

5. **Implementation** □

6. **Summative evaluation** □

a. The tested material is implemented with the target audience in the real environment.

b. We break down the topic into subordinate objectives and then group these into modules which can be taught together.

c. In this phase we clarify the performance problem and agree upon appropriate solutions.

d. The draft material is tested and improved.

e. The material is word processed, desktop published, or programmed.

f. We check the success of the training in solving the original performance problem.

Answers

Can you match the phrase with the appropriate definition?

1. **Analysis**   c

2. **Design**   b

3. **Development**   e

4. **Testing and improvement**   d

5. **Implementation**   a

6. **Summative evaluation**   f

a. **The tested material is implemented with the target audience in the real environment.**

b. **We break down the topic into subordinate objectives and then group these into modules which can be taught together.**

c. **In this phase we clarify the performance problem and agree upon appropriate solutions.**

d. **The draft material is tested and improved.**

e. **The material is word processed, desktop published, or programmed.**

f. **We check the success of the training in solving the original performance problem.**

How did you do?

If you are having problems, refer back to page 31.
Complete this quiz correctly before you move on.

Module 1 Analysis

- ***Unit 1***

  How to analyze a performance problem

- ***Unit 2***

  How to get inside the heads of your target group

- ***Unit 3***

  When is self-directed learning appropriate?

- ***Unit 4***

  How to get your subject matter expertise

Unit 1

How to analyze a
performance problem

Your customers will often come to you with a solution in mind. This is what we call ***solutioneering.***

It is important, for your own self-protection and to ensure a successful solution, that you find the real problem and appropriate solutions without making assumptions.

The steps in this unit allow you to analyze the cause of any performance problem. Interested?

Objective

By the end of this unit you will have analyzed all the possible causes for the performance problem in your project and have a list of necessary solutions.

What is performance analysis?

Pioneered by Robert Mager and Peter Pipe, this is a series of steps to find the cause of any performance problem and all the solutions needed to solve it, not just training.

A project to work on?

This book cannot cover the skill of designing effective self-directed learning. It can only give you a framework in which to work and some aids to performance. However, if you use it to work on a real project and get someone to give you feedback and guidance, you can start to develop your skill.

Choose a topic where you know enough about the people's performance concerned. Try a relatively simple one to start with.

Get some help!

The best way to learn is to get together with a colleague and work on the same topic. One of you needs to know enough about the subject matter to answer the other's questions.

Try to get someone to agree to support you in your learning, even if it is only someone with whom to discuss your answers. You can do it on your own but it is much better to get some help.

From now on you are going to work on your own project.

We have included an example of salespeople selling a mythical insurance product to doctors, called Doctors' Professional Insurance (DPI).

Your project

If you haven't got a project, stop reading and go and get one!

What is the title of your project?

e.g.   **Doctors' Professional Insurance (DPI)**

1. **Briefly describe the problem**

    e.g.   **Information and marketing material is scarce and the salesforce is not selling enough of this sophisticated product**

2. **Describe who is involved**

    e.g.   **Experienced salespeople and service representatives**

A system diagram

3. Sometimes it helps to draw a diagram of everyone involved in the problem, i.e. the system.

   Put a line around the main players involved in the performance that you want to do something about.

   Try drawing a system diagram for your project.

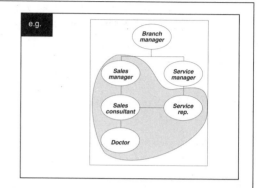

4. **Describe what the main people are doing at the moment (the existing performance)**

    e.g.   *Only a few salespeople are selling this product at the moment*
                Service reps are not passing on any leads
                Branches are not hitting targets for sales. Company sells $500,000 this year (25% of target)

5. **Describe what your customer wants them to be doing (the desired performance)**

    e.g.   *All salespeople can sell this product*
                Company sales target of $2 million achieved for DPI

6. **How will your customer know when they can do this?**

    e.g.   *All salespeople pass the test and are qualified to sell DPI*
                Annual sales targets achieved for all regions for DPI

What are the causes of the performance gap?

Reasons for poor performance are usually a combination of the following, in this order:

- **Poor information/unclear expectations**
- **Difficult environment/inadequate equipment**
- **Poor incentives**
- **Lack of knowledge**
- **Lack of skills**
- **Poor motivation**

Source: Thomas F. Gilbert *The Behaviour Engineering Model* 1978.

Note that 'performance gap' does not imply deficiencies in people. Most people want to do a good job.

What we can tackle with training is the lack of knowledge and skills. But how do we deal with the other causes of low performance?

First, let's quantify the problem a bit more...

7. Now describe the effect of doing nothing

    e.g.   Sales will remain static, branches will not meet targets

8. Finally, estimate the cost of the gap if it remains

    e.g.   Lose potential sales of $1.5 million

           Company will fail to establish itself in an expanding market

9. Is it worth doing something about?

[Questions adapted from Mager and Pipe's
Analysing Performance Problems 1990]

What solutions could close this gap?

We could:

- **provide better information**
- **improve the environment, equipment, etc.**
- **provide better incentives**
- **reduce the task**
- **provide performance aids, e.g., checklists, diagrams, flowcharts, etc.**
- **provide practice, feedback, and coaching**
- **encourage on-the-job training**
- **provide training**

Training is last on the list because it is expensive. Often simpler, more effective solutions can be found.

The danger of only implementing a training solution is that it may fail to achieve the desired performance because it fails to address other key causes for the performance gap!

Customers often have unrealistic expectations of training solutions (virtually setting them up to fail). If you are finding it difficult to meet all these expectations then it is probable that there was inadequate analysis of the causes of low performance in the first place.

On the following pages is a superb performance aid. Use it to analyze the causes of the performance gap and generate ideas for solutions. List all the possible solutions in the spaces provided.

The Ideas Generator ACT Consultants *Solving Performance Problems Workbook 1998 (based on Mager and Pipe's performance analysis flowchart, 1979)*

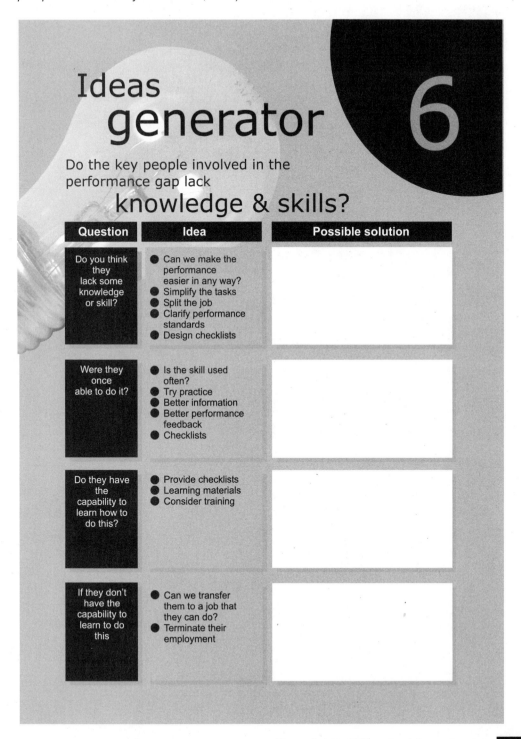

Ideas **generator** **6**

Do the key people involved in the performance gap lack
knowledge & skills?

Question	Idea	Possible solution
Do you think they lack some knowledge or skill?	● Can we make the performance easier in any way? ● Simplify the tasks ● Split the job ● Clarify performance standards ● Design checklists	
Were they once able to do it?	● Is the skill used often? ● Try practice ● Better information ● Better performance feedback ● Checklists	
Do they have the capability to learn how to do this?	● Provide checklists ● Learning materials ● Consider training	
If they don't have the capability to learn to do this	● Can we transfer them to a job that they can do? ● Terminate their employment	

6

Do the key people involved in the performance gap lack

motivation?

Question	Idea	Possible solution
Do they get insufficient feedback on performance?	● Provide clear individual performance goals ● Regular feedback on positive and negative performance	
If they do it right, do they suffer, e.g., By being given more work?	● Reduce the punishment for high performance ● Introduce rewards and incentives ● Make rewards based on performance	
If they do it wrong, do they benefit, e.g., by being left alone?	● Stop rewards for low performance ● Increase the incentive for doing it right	
Does it really matter to them?	● Make it matter! ● Talk to them ● Clarify the expectations of the job ● Set goals ● Set up measurement, provide honest feedback ● Help people envision successful outcomes	
Is there a fear of failure?	● Agree on realistic goals ● Give them a range to aim for ● Tell them that you know they are trying their best and that problems will be dealt with supportively	

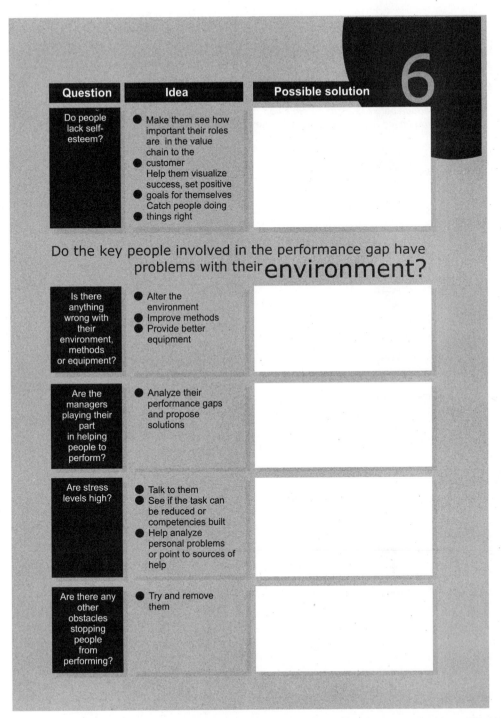

Question	Idea	Possible solution
Do people lack self-esteem?	● Make them see how important their roles are in the value chain to the customer ● Help them visualize success, set positive goals for themselves ● Catch people doing things right	

Do the key people involved in the performance gap have problems with their environment?

Question	Idea	Possible solution
Is there anything wrong with their environment, methods or equipment?	● Alter the environment ● Improve methods ● Provide better equipment	
Are the managers playing their part in helping people to perform?	● Analyze their performance gaps and propose solutions	
Are stress levels high?	● Talk to them ● See if the task can be reduced or competencies built ● Help analyze personal problems or point to sources of help	
Are there any other obstacles stopping people from performing?	● Try and remove them	

6

List all the solutions and estimate how much each will cost. Suspend judgment as to their feasibility.

e.g.	*Improve marketing brochures*	*20k*
	Train all sales consultants in DPI	*100k*
	Introduce better rates of commission	*self-funding*
	Train service reps to spot opportunities	*30k*

Reality

Get together with your partner, and eliminate the solutions that fail this reality filter:

• Are any impossible to implement?
• Is the cost greater than the benefit?

Highlight those which:

• we can easily implement
• will give us best results for minimum effort

Which solutions are you left with?

e.g. Ask marketing to improve marketing brochures and introduce better rates of commission   20k

While we:

start to design a training program to improve the performance of the sales teams, i.e., all sales staff and service reps

---

Action plan

What do we need to do next?

e.g. Contact marketing and find out what plans they have to improve the material. Start to design a training program to improve the performance of sales teams	Who	When

If this is how to analyze a performance problem, what is a Training Needs Analysis?

Training Needs Analysis (TNA) is an inaccurate term because **training** never has **needs**. Only **people** have needs. Training is a 'how to' to achieve something else, not an end in itself.

However, you can safely assume that there is a need for training when it is a **new performance** and you know that the target group does not have the knowledge and skills to perform it.

Even then it is dangerous to think in terms of a Training Needs Analysis because you might shut out alternative solutions other than the training group's needs. TNA is dangerous! **Always think performance analysis**. Not training!

So what do I do when I believe training is part of the solution?

When you have isolated parts of the problem that can be tackled by training, i.e., those that need knowledge and skill, you can safely write a final objective for the training element of the solution, e.g.:

All salespeople pass the license test on the knowledge and skills required to sell DPI.

What about improving and maintaining existing performance?

We have covered how to solve specific performance problems and shown that training is appropriate for those in new roles, but what about maintaining existing performance?

In this case the target group probably has the knowledge and skills to do the job so the biggest impact on continuing performance is **organizational issues.**

Can I handle this by training?

Not really!

If it is a complex organizational problem you are probably better off bringing in a performance consultant. Training can only really tackle knowledge and skill shortfalls comfortably. For complex culture and behavior change, bring in the experts and you will probably find yourself working as a team with these experts.

What you can do, however, is to design powerful visions into your materials and sell the benefits of achieving the objectives to the learner, so some motivation is built into the material.

The clearer, shorter, more relevant to the learner that you make the learning material, the better.

Write an aim or objective for the training part of your project

   e.g.   By the end of the training, salespeople will be able to pass the license test and prove that they
   can sell DPI in training scenarios

Summary

How to analyze a performance problem

- If a customer is trying to "***solutioneer,***" start by asking them:

    - Who is involved?
    - What are they doing now?
    - What do you want them to do?

- Then move on to find out more about the reasons for the gap:

    - Poor information/unclear expectations
    - Difficult environment/inadequate equipment
    - Poor incentives
    - Lack of knowledge
    - Lack of skills
    - Poor motivation

- Use the Ideas Generator to list all solutions

- Put these through a reality filter

- Extract the knowledge and skill element that you can tackle with training

- Write an objective for the training element (if any)

Unit 2

How to get inside the heads of your target group

Objective

By the end of this unit you will be able to:

* *state the difference between target population and target group*
* *describe the target group for your project*
* *name three of the five questions that you might use to describe your target group*

What is the difference between target population and target group?

The target population for your project is **all the people who may use it,** e.g., from sales manager to sales representative. However, you cannot design the course with the needs of a number of people in mind. So you need to 'target' the **main users of the solution,** say salespeople, and aim it at them. The target group is usually the **largest** group or the **most important in influencing the desired performance.**

The rest of your target population will be able to use the course but you will have stated that it was not designed for them.

If you do not define your target group clearly then you will run into problems with the design. Examples which may be ideal for supervisors will not suit managers or support staff. If you do not state who you designed the course for, then you leave yourself open to criticism.

You may be able to cope with different groups by producing different versions of the same course, so that people can see what is in the course without needing to work all the way through it.

Describe the target group of your project using the checklist on the following pages

Remember, these are only prompts. Ignore questions that do not work for you.

Think back to our system diagram

The most important person who is in contact with the customer and affects the end result (DPI sales) is the salesperson.

Sales consultants form the target group.

Who is in the target population?
e.g. *Sales managers, salespeople, doctors, service reps are all in the target population*

Who is in the target group?
e.g. *Salespeople*

The quality and the effectiveness of your learning package will depend on how well you can 'get into the head' of the learner.

For example, what you find out here will influence your screen designs. Will they be set in the workshop or on the battlefield? Would your target group appreciate cartoons or not?

It all depends on how well you understand what motivates your target group.

This is what we found out about our salespeople.

2500 staff located in all 50 states

20% annual staff turnover

Age 24-35, 65% male, 35% female

Base salary $28,000 + commission. Top performers will earn over $100k

Most are college-leavers

Many have had previous sales jobs

Most have been asking for improved training and marketing material

Very busy in evenings with sales calls. Have some free time during the day. Most offices have conference rooms which could be used for training rooms. Are very interested in doing anything which will increase the amount of products they can sell and earn them more commission. Junior staff will follow examples set by the top performers.

Very status- and money-conscious.

Highly motivated by fear of failing. Many have access to a laptop computer.

General

Job title

Background

Experience

Attitudes

Have people asked for training?

Have people had training before?

How did they react?

Do people prefer to set aside time for training all at once, or to find the time in small chunks?

Do people prefer to go away for training?

Do people associate training with formal, school-like methods?

What would encourage people to take part in training?

What other activities would compete with training time?

What are people's attitudes toward their work?

How do people change courses to make them more enjoyable for themselves?

What unrealistic preconceptions might they have about training?

What training or learning materials have worked well for this group in the past?

Education

What experience of formal education and training do people have?

Are they comfortable with computers?

What motivates your target group?

What would people count as an achievement?

What do people mean by 'I am a success'?

Whose good opinions or respect do they value?

What things do people think affect their standing with their peers?

Interests

What do they do when not working?

What do they talk about?

What could hinder their learning?

Can people concentrate? For how long?

Where are they?

Do they work from home?

Do they spend a lot of time travelling?

Quiz

1. **What is the difference between a target population and a target group?**

   A target population is:

   A target group is:

2. **Have you described the target group for your project?**

   ✓

   No

   Yes

3. **From memory, name at least five questions that you might use to get inside the heads of a target group**

   1.

   2.

   3.

   4.

   5.

Answers

1. What is the difference between a target population and a target group?

   A target population is:

   > **All the people who may use it**

   A target group is:

   > **The main users for the solution; usually the largest**
   > **or most important group**

2. Have you described the target group for your project?

   No → Do it! If you cannot answer the questions, go and ask someone who knows the target group

   Yes ↓ Move on to Unit 3

3. From memory, name at least five questions that you might use to get inside the heads of a target group

   > 1.   Check with pages 62 and 63
   >
   > 2.
   >
   > 3.
   >
   > 4.
   >
   > 5.

Unit 3

When is self-directed learning appropriate?

Objective

By the end of this unit, given a need to assess the feasibility of a self-directed learning project, you will be able to find a checklist of key factors which indicate that self-directed learning may be an effective solution.

When is self-directed learning appropriate?

Use this checklist to see if self-directed learning is appropriate for your project

	e.g., financial salespeople	your project
	Yes/No	
Do you have a large target group? So that you can justify the large one-off investment	Yes	
Are they geographically dispersed? They would find training courses difficult to get to	Yes	
Is the training to be repeated often? Either for new starters or refresher training	No	
Does the material have a decent shelf-life? So there will not be many updates	Yes	
Will people enter training with variable levels of skill and knowledge?	No	

If you answered yes to most items above, self-directed learning may help.

However, do your learners have the required:

• literacy?	Yes	
• study skills?	?	
• self-discipline?	?	
• confidence?	?	
• motivation?	Yes	

Could your learners benefit significantly from these features?

	e.g., financial salespeople	your project
	Yes/No	
They can learn at their own pace, place, and time	Yes	
It doesn't have the negative associations that traditional classroom teaching might have	Yes	
It can help link training to work because you can do it at work and use real projects and exercises to work from	Yes	

Is self-directed learning appropriate for your project?

Why?

e.g.   *It is probably the only thing that will work for this highly motivated but dispersed group of salespeople who have spare time during the day because most current sales are made in the evening*

What support do I need to plan for?

Support for learners from colleagues, line managers, and tutors is vital. You plan for this in your design by identifying such people in your system diagram and target audience. You will probably have to produce some training for them on how to offer their support. But don't worry about this now, wait until the materials are being tested to assess what you will need.

Unit 4

How to get your subject matter expertise

Objective

> **By the end of this unit you will be able to identify:**
>
> - *a high performer*
> - *a subject matter expert (SME)*
> - *a signatory for your project*

Existing material

Now you know who your target group is and roughly what it needs to be able to do (the desired performance). You have enough information to find out whether any of the material you need already exists. This need not necessarily be material that you can use directly, but anything that covers part of the subject or gives you ideas for approaches to use.

Note below any existing material that could be used for all or part of your project
e.g.   Existing marketing material on DPI

You will need access to local expertise to help you design your solutions.

No one person will have all the required knowledge and skills for the complete training package. Identify your experts and involve them now.

Someone who can do the job well already, your high performer
e.g.   *Tracey Shaw, Salesperson of the Year*

> **Name**

An expert in the subject, your subject matter expert (SME)
e.g.   *D'Lyn Washington, Technical Director, Medical Insurance*

> **Name** .

A representative sample of the target group
e.g.   *Mid-West sales team*

>

Signatories: individuals who sign off on the project stages, the customer who has to approve the final product
e.g.   *John Ballard, Marketing Director (customer), Jane Jordan, Compliance*

> **Names**

Quiz

	Yes/No
1. **Have you identified a high performer?**	☐
2. **Have you identified SMEs for all topics?**	☐
3. **Have you identified a sample of your target group?**	☐
4. **Have you defined who your customer is?**	☐

You should have done all the above before proceeding

Summary

ANALYSIS CHECKLIST

Have you:

Defined the problem as you see it..☐
Drawn a system diagram...☐
Identified the target group...☐
Described the existing performance..☐
Described the desired performance..☐
Estimated the value of the performance gap $......................................☐
Described the effect of doing nothing...☐
Investigated existing material...☐
Listed all the possible solutions...☐
Identified own recommended solutions...☐
Identified: High performers...☐
                    Subject matter experts......................................☐
                    Target group sample..☐
                    Sign off...☐

Listed the action needed

Action	Who	When

Module 2 Design

- ### *Unit 1*

How to write measurable objectives

- ### *Unit 2*

Pyramid analysis

- ### *Unit 3*

Selecting appropriate media

- ### *Unit 4*

Starting the detailed design

- ### *Unit 5*

Test question design

Unit 1

How to write measurable objectives

Objective

> *By the end of this unit you will be able to:*
>
> - *describe the two ways that objectives are used in designing self-directed and distance learning*
> - *state the four elements of a measurable performance objective*
> - *state the phrase used to check whether an objective is measurable*
> - *write a measurable objective for your project*

Objectives are used in two ways in self-directed learning

1.   Design objectives

This is designers' shorthand for all the elements that need to go into a successful design. They may be written in a long-winded, technical way.

2.   Learner's objectives

This is a motivating statement of what the learner will be able to do at the end of any unit of training. It is written in a friendly and inspiring way to help the learner to visualize himself or herself carrying out the performance.

Measurable learning objectives are the key to effective training

Many so-called objectives are aims. For example:

'The objective of the seminar is that the students will gain an understanding of the manufacturing process.'

This is not an objective **because it is not measurable.**

There are four elements to a good objective:

Conditions

e.g., by the side of the road

Performance

e.g., change a wheel

Standards

e.g., within 15 minutes

Method of assessment

e.g., timed by passenger's watch

This method of splitting objectives into elements was pioneered by Robert Mager (see *Preparing Instructional Objectives,* Mager, 1962), although he uses 'criterion' to describe standards and method of assessment.

Objectives checklist

Conditions

| |
| |

Are they realistic? ☐

Performance

| |
| |

Can you ask 'Watch me'? ☐

Standards

| |
| |

Are they measurable? ☐

Are they appropriate? ☐

Method of assessment

| |
| |

Specified? ☐

The elements in more detail

Conditions - a performance always happens under certain conditions

The nearer these conditions are to the actual situation, the better they will be. For example, it is one thing to be able to change a flat tire in a warm, well-lit garage, but quite another to do the same task in the middle of the night by the side of the road. On the other hand, a trainee engineer will not be able to learn to repair a piece of equipment on the site unless he or she can first learn to repair it in the workshop. So conditions are used either to limit, or to enlarge, what a learner has to do: they must be *realistic.*

Performance - what the learner will be able to do

The performance must be observable. Words such as 'understand,' 'appreciate,' 'know' are useless. We cannot see anyone 'appreciating.' So use verbs of action. If you have any doubts, place 'watch me' before the verb describing the performance.

'Watch me ... understand this software.'
'Watch me ... use a spreadsheet to produce a cash flow.'

Make sure that the verb in your objective is the *desired performance* you had in mind.

Standards - how well must this performance be done?

- Standards must be *measurable* and *attainable*
- Set them too low and they will not be effective; too high and they will be demotivating, so start with a first stab and get them right by testing
- Standards must be appropriate for the topic, e.g., safety standards may require a 100 percent success rate. If an accident occurs, you may not get a second chance to do the task more carefully
- Always consider the level of performance needed in real life

Method of assessment - what method will you use to assess?

Robert Mager stresses that we must specify the method of assessment as part of the standard, e.g., Is it by the supervisor using a checklist or by a computer-based quiz? It makes a difference.

Example objective

Use the checklist to analyze the following objective:

> **Use PC payroll with training data to print a payroll summary,
> so that your supervisor signs off that it matches the example given exactly.**

1   *Look for the conditions*

'PC payroll with training data.'

2   *Look for the performance*

'Use PC payroll to print a payroll summary' describes what someone has to do.

3   *Check for the standards*

'Matches the example given exactly.'

4   *Has the method of assessment been specified?*

'Supervisor signs.'

This example contains the four elements of a good objective.

You should now be able to check any statement that claims to be an objective to see whether it contains these vital elements.

Objectives checklist

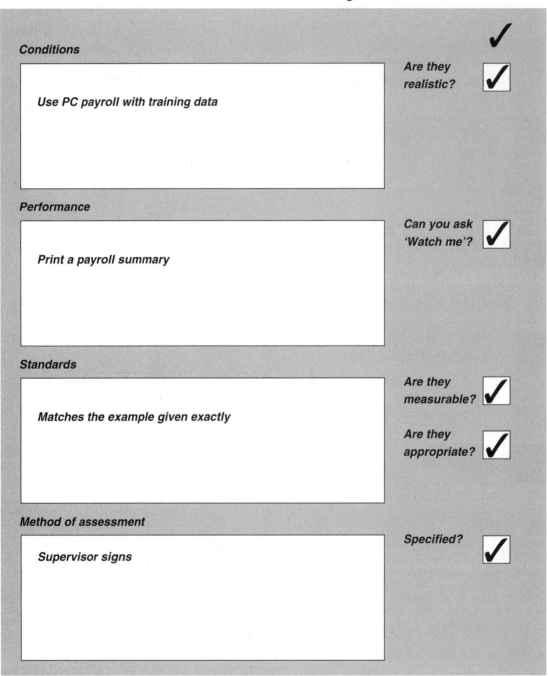

Conditions

Use PC payroll with training data

Are they realistic?

Performance

Print a payroll summary

Can you ask 'Watch me'?

Standards

Matches the example given exactly

Are they measurable?

Are they appropriate?

Method of assessment

Supervisor signs

Specified?

Objectives for practice

Given the following four objectives, analyze each one using a blank checklist for each.

Check your answers after each attempt using the 'Check Yourself' sheets.

Your analysis should match ours (this is the only standard for this exercise, as you are still learning). If you have any difficulty, talk it over with a colleague.

---

1. **Given the example data entry forms, set up the stock, supplier, and customer files and obtain a printout, so that the printout matches the entry form exactly.**

2. **By the time you complete this workbook you will be able to develop your skills in all areas of customer service.**

3. **From the user manual, identify correctly all five of the following components:**

   (a)   mother board
   (b)   fan
   (c)   power supply
   (d)   daughter boards
   (e)   disk drives

4. **With a set of tools, and the reference manual, adjust the display to the correct focus, so that a set of 'Hs' appears sharp to your instructor.**

Given the example data entry forms, set up the stock, supplier, and customer files and obtain a printout, so that the printout matches the entry form exactly.

Practice 1

Conditions

Are they realistic? ☐ ✔

Performance

Can you ask 'Watch me'? ☐

Standards

Are they measurable? ☐

Are they appropriate? ☐

Method of assessment

Specified? ☐

Given the example data entry forms, set up the stock, supplier, and customer files and obtain a printout, so that the printout matches the entry form exactly.

Answers

Conditions

Given the example data and the entry forms

Are they realistic? ✓

Performance

Set up the stock, supplier, and customer files and obtain a printout

Can you ask 'Watch me'? ✓

Standards

So that the printout matches the entry form exactly

Are they measurable? ✓

Are they appropriate? ✓

Method of assessment

Specified? ✗

2

By the time you complete this workbook you will be able to develop your skills in all areas of customer service.

Practice 2

✔

Conditions

Are they realistic?

Performance

Can you ask 'Watch me'?

Standards

Are they measurable?

Are they appropriate?

Method of assessment

Specified?

2 By the time you complete this workbook you will be able to develop your skills in all areas of customer service.

Answers

Conditions

✔

By the time you complete this workbook

Are they realistic? ?

Performance

You will be able to develop your skills in all areas of customer service

Can you ask 'Watch me'? ✗

Standards

Are they measurable? ✗

Are they appropriate? ✗

Method of assessment

Specified? ✗

From the user manual, identify correctly all five of the following components:
(a) mother board (b) fan (c) power supply
(d) daughter boards (e) disk drives

Practice 3

Conditions

✓

Are they
realistic?

Performance

Can you ask
'Watch me'?

Standards

Are they
measurable?

Are they
appropriate?

Method of assessment

Specified?

From the user manual, identify correctly all five of the following components:
(a) mother board (b) fan (c) power supply
(d) daughter boards (e) disk drives

Answers

Conditions

From the user manual

Are they
realistic? ✓

Performance

Identify all five of the following components:
(a) mother board (b) fan (c) power supply
(d) daughter boards (e) disk drives

Can you ask
'Watch me'? ✓

Standards

All five, correctly

Are they
measurable? ✓

Are they
appropriate? ?

Method of assessment

Specified? X

With a set of tools, and the reference manual, adjust the display to the correct focus, so that a set of 'Hs' appears sharp to your supervisor.

Practice 4

Conditions

✓

	Are they realistic? ☐

Performance

Can you ask 'Watch me'? ☐

Standards

Are they measurable? ☐

Are they appropriate? ☐

Method of assessment

Specified? ☐

With a set of tools, and the reference manual, adjust the
display to the correct focus, so that a set of 'Hs' appears
sharp to your supervisor.

Answers

Conditions

Given a set of tools, and the reference manual

Are they
realistic? ✓ ✓

Performance

Adjust the display

Can you ask
'Watch me'? ✓

Standards

To the correct focus

Are they
measurable? ✓

Are they
appropriate? ✓

Method of assessment

So that a set of 'Hs' appears sharp to your supervisor

Specified? ✓

Quiz

1. Describe the two ways that objectives are used in self-directed learning.

2. What are the four elements of good objectives?

1.

2.

3.

4.

3. What phrase is used in front of the verb to check whether a performance is observable?

4. Analyze this objective:
On completion of this unit you will have a good knowledge of safety regulations when working underground.

Answers

1. **Describe the two ways that objectives are used in self-directed learning.**

   Design objectives   -   **Shorthand design for the designer**

   Learner's objectives   -   **Friendly description of what the learner will be able to do**

2. **What are the four elements of good objectives?**

   1. Conditions

   2. Performance

   3. Standards

   4. Method of assessment

3. **What phrase is used in front of the verb to check whether a performance is observable?**

   'Watch me'

4. **Analyze this objective:**
   On completion of this unit you will have a good knowledge of safety regulations when working underground.

   Conditions
   On completion of this unit. **The conditions are precise**

   Performance
   You will have a good knowledge of safety regulations when working underground.
   But they are meaningless because the performance is not observable.

   Standards   **A better objective might be:**
   No standards have been set.   *On completion of this unit you will be able to answer accurately and without hesitation 10 questions on the underground safety*
   Method of assessment   *regulations to your safety office.*
   None

Now write a performance objective.

This comes straight from the desired performance.

e.g.　　　*A performance objective for insurance salespeople*

Example

Conditions

Given eight interviews with doctors over six months, accompanied by your sales manager

Are they realistic?

Performance

- *complete the DPI fact-find*
- *outline the benefits of DPI*
- *overcome common obstacles*
- *close the sale*

Can you ask 'Watch me'?

Standards

No technical errors in the fact-find
so that you make the sale in 80 percent of cases with an identified need

Are they measurable?

Are they appropriate?

Method of assessment

Fact-find checked by technical officer

Sales manager evaluates closing rate for each accompanied sale. Achievement of standard will lead to license to sell DPI

Specified?

Now write a performance objective for your project

Write the performance objective for your project.

What is the difference between a performance objective and a training objective?

Very little. You will see from our example that **the main changes are the conditions.** We cannot use real interviews so we use role-plays.

The rule is to **keep as close to the real conditions** as possible, e.g.,

Given eight multimedia role-play simulations of interviews with doctors:

> **Salespeople will complete the DPI fact-find, outline the benefits of DPI, overcome common obstacles, close the sales**
>
> **so that you make the sale in 80 percent of cases with an identified need**
>
> **and the computer rates your performance as satisfactory using a checklist**
>
> **Achievement of the standard will lead to a provisional license to sell DPI in accompanied sales**

On the next page, write a final training objective for your own project.

* Make sure it conforms to the standards set out in the checklist
* Show your objectives to a colleague

In the next unit we will see how to break down the topic into the subordinate or enabling objectives needed to achieve this final objective.

The training objective for my project

Conditions

<table>
<tr><td></td><td>Are they realistic?</td><td>☐</td></tr>
</table>

Performance

Can you ask 'Watch me'? ☐

Standards

Are they measurable? ☐

Are they appropriate? ☐

Method of assessment

Specified? ☐

Unit 2

Pyramid analysis

The objective you have written is the final objective for your project. The next step is to split up the topic into manageable chunks using a technique called *pyramid analysis.*

Objective

By the end of this unit, given your project's final objective, you will be able to draw a pyramid of objectives.

(All the prerequisite knowledge and skills should be marked on the pyramid.)

Pyramid analysis is an invaluable technique that allows you to **split a topic up into manageable chunks.** These chunks can then be combined into modules. You can then decide the order in which they are to be presented and which medium to use.

It is a skill that needs practice.

Pyramids also help you to make sure that everything you should have included in your design is present. The best way to do this is to **start with your final objective and work downward.** Then you can be sure that everything you identify is essential to reaching that final objective and not just something you think it would be good for the learner to know. What you are actually doing is dividing a final objective into its subordinate or enabling objectives.

How to draw a pyramid

Take the final objective for your project and write this on the top of a large piece of paper.

Then ask the question:

'What does a person need to be able to do in order to do this?'

The answers go on the next level of your pyramid.

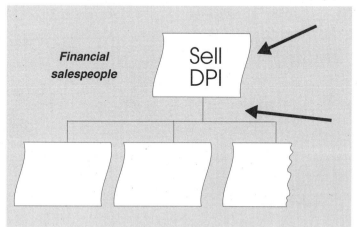

A short version of your final objective

Financial salespeople

Sell DPI

Ask the question 'What does the target group need to be able to do in order to do this?'

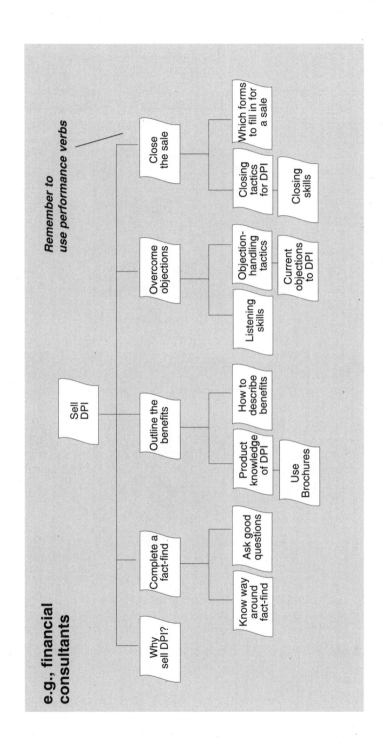

Helpful hints

1. Draw your pyramid with the guidance of a high performer (someone you have identified who can do the task well).
2. Use a large piece of paper and set aside at least one hour.
3. Use small Post-it Notes, so that you can move topics around. (You never get it right the first time.)

4. Write your objectives in shorthand form to try to keep the *real* words used by the high performer, e.g.:

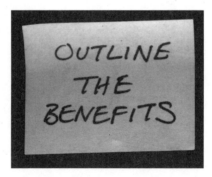

5. Don't worry too much if it doesn't make much sense at the beginning.
   As long as you have the information on Post-it Notes you can always move it around later.

6. Once you have a rough pyramid, take it to another high performer and your subject matter expert (SME) and improve it. You will find that having the information on Post-it Notes helps.

Prerequisite knowledge and skills

Now that you have a pyramid of all the knowledge and skills needed to achieve the objective, you may be able to specify some topics as prerequisites for your course. For example, we don't want to cover listening skills or generic closing skills so we indicate these as prerequisites by a dotted line on our pyramid.

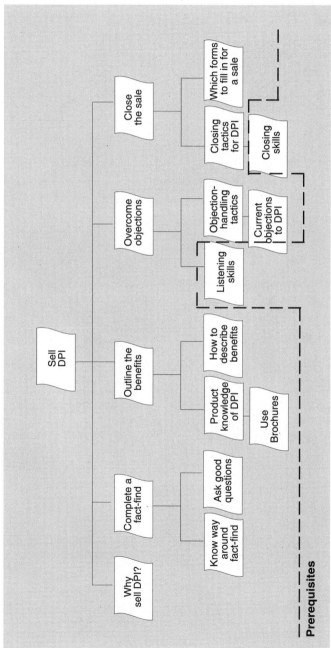

Group topics into modules

Now you have a pyramid. You can arrange topics together into groups that you can tackle at the same time.

There is no science to this. Just put things together that seem to involve similar performances. Use a pen to draw circles around common topics.

- Big groups will be modules
- Sub-groups will be units

Structure

We use the following:

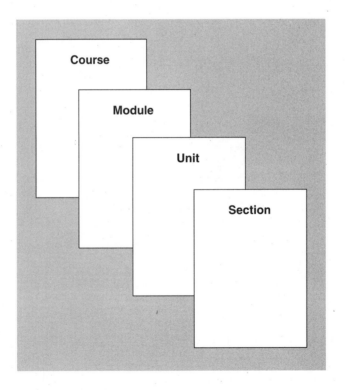

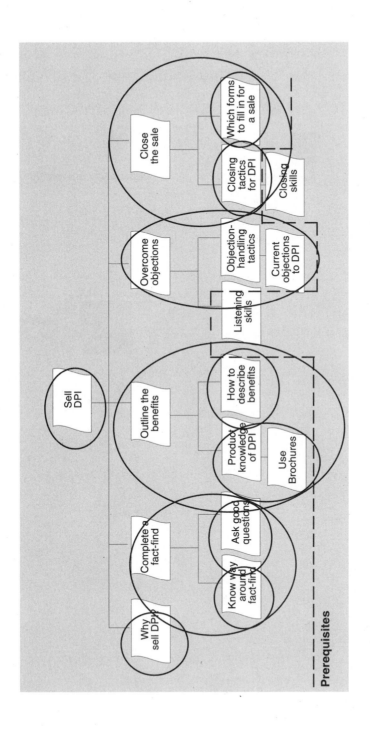

Order of learning

Annotate your diagram with module and unit numbers:

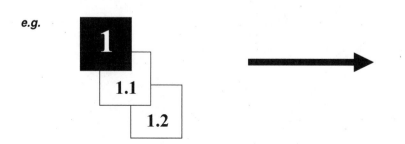

Don't forget that the final objective may be a module itself, usually the final exercise or test for the course.

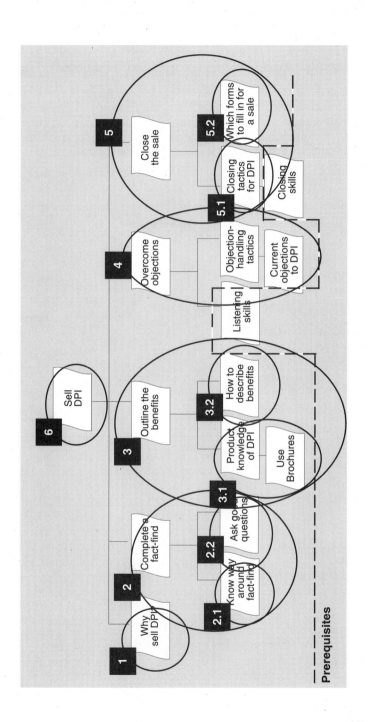

A learning map

So far, pyramids have been used for our purposes, as course designers (and they can get pretty messy). Now that you have an order of modules, you can represent them for the learner.

Redraw your modules on a learning map, see page 117.

By convention, we start at the bottom and build up. Notice how the modules retain their active performance titles, like 'How to ...' This keeps the topic alive. Notice also how modules can be of different sizes to represent importance or amount of content.

N.B. Short-term memory will hold about nine items. This means that we can hold a pattern of nine things in our heads. So make your course nine or fewer modules in length and represent them in a diagram.

There are two examples of real pyramids on pages 117 and 118.

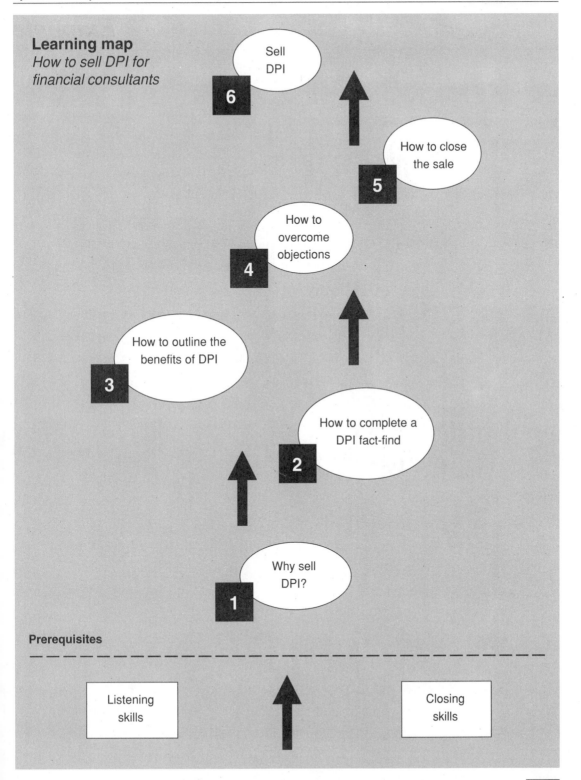

Learning map
How to sell DPI for financial consultants

Sell DPI — 6

How to close the sale — 5

How to overcome objections — 4

How to outline the benefits of DPI — 3

How to complete a DPI fact-find — 2

Why sell DPI? — 1

Prerequisites

Listening skills

Closing skills

Example

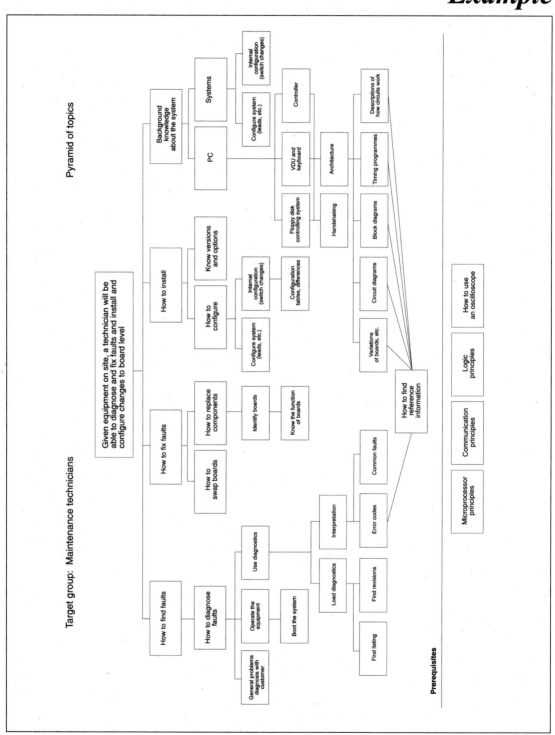

Pyramid of topics

Target group: Maintenance technicians

Given equipment on site, a technician will be able to diagnose and fix faults and install and configure changes to board level

Background knowledge about the system
- Systems
  - Internal configuration (switch changes)
  - Configure system (leads, etc.)
- PC
  - Controller
  - VDU and keyboard
  - Architecture
  - Floppy disk controlling system
  - Handshaking
  - Descriptions of how circuits work
  - Timing programmes
  - Block diagrams

How to install
- Know versions and options
- How to configure
  - Internal configuration (switch changes)
  - Configuration tables, differences
  - Configure system (leads, etc.)
  - Circuit diagrams

How to fix faults
- How to replace components
  - Identify boards
  - Know the function of boards
- How to swap boards
- Variations of boards, etc.

How to find faults
- How to diagnose faults
  - Use diagnostics
    - Interpretation
    - Common faults
    - Error codes
  - Operate the equipment
  - Load diagnostics
  - Find revisions
  - Boot the system
  - General problems diagnosis with customer
  - Find listing

How to find reference information

Prerequisites
- Microprocessor principles
- Communication principles
- Logic principles
- How to use an oscilloscope

Summary

Drawing pyramids using a large piece of paper and Post-it Notes is a very creative way of getting your high performers and SMEs involved in the project. As you work together on the pyramid design you can 'see' the structure of the training emerge in front of your eyes. It can be very rewarding.

Now, on the following blank page, create a pyramid of topics for your project and include prerequisites.

Remember:

• What does a person need to be able to do in order to do this?

• Use one small Post-it Note for each topic. (It will save you a lot of erasing.)

That is the end of this unit of pyramid analysis.

Unit 3

Selecting appropriate media

Have you ever been confused about learning types, cognitive versus psychomotor, how to cope with learning styles? What is the best training method to use? Is multimedia better than classroom training? This unit answers these questions.

Objective

By the end of this unit you will be able to:

* *demonstrate the two fundamentally different types of learning*
* *list the advantages and disadvantages of different types of media*
* *state what media-effective instruction always involves*
* *name the method that you always consider first*
* *make a list of performance aids used in everyday life*
* *state three of the four reasons for using performance aids*

The two fundamental types of learning are:

You need to know this because the way people learn skills is different from the way they acquire knowledge and this will affect your choice of medium on your learning map.

The difference is that skill can only be learned by **practice** and **feedback**, e.g., you might acquire the basic knowledge about how to kick a football, but you can only develop skill by trying it and getting feedback.

Knowledge can be acquired at a distance using books, etc., but skill needs practice.

Check for the potential to use performance aids

The next essential step in the design process is to consider the potential for using performance aids, like the performance analysis flowchart.

A performance aid can often reduce the training needed and so is very cost-effective. You use them:

1. To jog memory

   e.g.   checklists, labels,
          diagrams, codes,
          mnemonics

2. To improve information

   e.g.   different kinds of signals,
          automatic reminders, rules,
          blocking information that is
          not essential, feedback

3. To reduce complexity

   e.g.   calculators, tables,
          algorithms, procedures,
          graphs, decision trees,
          simulations, printed formats

4. To identify something quickly

   e.g.   colors, labels, shapes

Save money with performance aids

Using performance aids can reduce or remove the need for training altogether.

In one case a company replaced a lesson on how to start up and shut down machinery with a table of color-coded instructions which were stuck on each machine!

In another case of a new version of software, additional help screens and on-screen prompts removed the need for training altogether.

Exercise

We use performance aids all the time in everyday life.

List as many as you can think of, then compare them with our list on the next page.

Performance aids in everyday life:

Some examples of performance aids:

- the fill-line on a coffee maker

- road signs

- procedures

- quick reference cards

- templates on computer keyboards explaining function keys

- tables on the outside of washing machine powder drawers

- visual displays on photocopiers which tell you what to do

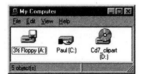

- icons on a computer screen

- pilot's checklists

- shaped plugs which will only fit into the correct socket

- colored casing for electrical wiring

- the NYC subway map

Examples

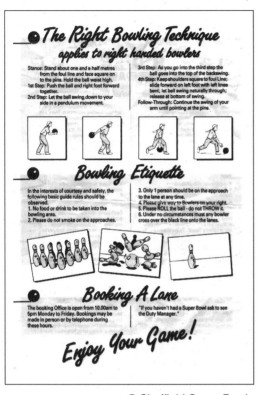

© Sheffield Super Bowl

before you

hand anything over **or** send anything out

Make sure you have:

Spell checked it ☐

Checked the grammar and punctuation ☐

Checked the layout ☐

Used the template ☐

Complied with text standards ☐

Checked the design and read it through ☐

Made all necessary edits ☐

Quality is ...

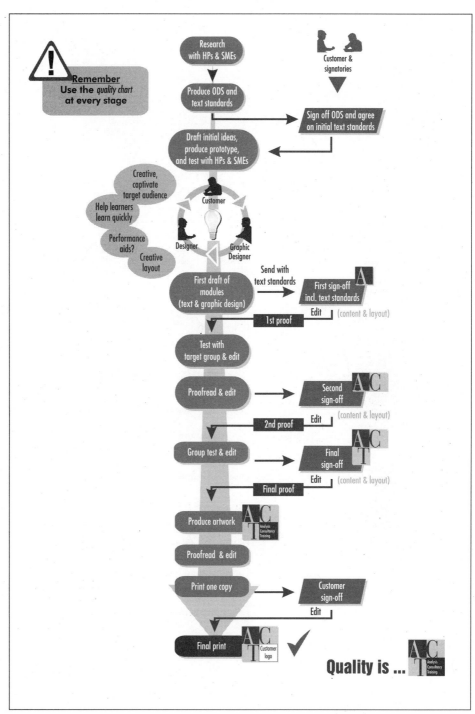

©1998 ACT Consultants Ltd.

Example

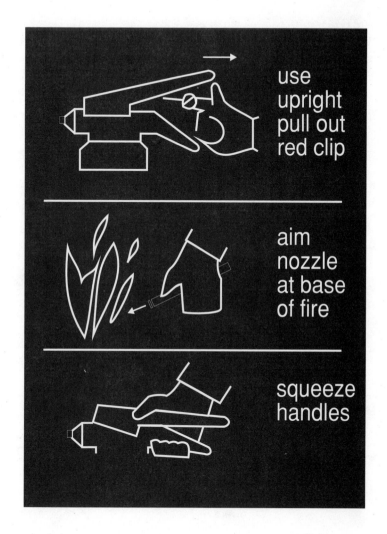

use
upright
pull out
red clip

aim
nozzle
at base
of fire

squeeze
handles

Fire Extinguisher

Use the power of graphics in your designs

The best statistical graphic?

Charles Joseph Minard (1781-1870) showed the devastating losses suffered in Napoleon's Russian campaign of 1812. In the chart below, beginning at the left on the Polish-Russian border, the thick band shows the size of the army. In September the army reached Moscow, which by then was sacked and deserted, with

100,000 men. The path of Napoleon's retreat is shown by the darker, lower band, which is linked to the temperature scale and dates at the bottom of the chart. It was a bitterly cold winter, and many froze on the march out of Russia. The army finally struggled back into Poland with only 10,000 men.

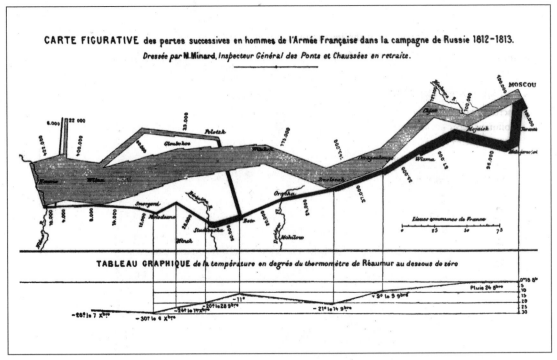

© *Edward R. Tufte, The Visual Display of Quantitative Information*
(Cheshire, Connecticut: Graphics Press, 1983)

This may be the best statistical graphic ever drawn, and shows how information can be more effectively transferred by graphics rather than text. Remember it when you come to design your pages and performance aids.

Pros and cons of different media

Now that you have a learning map, divided into modules, you have enough information to select the appropriate medium and instructional method for each module.

This makes nonsense of all those requests for 'a CBT course' or 'a video on...' You will often have a mixture of media. And you can use the advantages of some media to overcome the disadvantages of others.

You probably know most of them already. Make a note of the pros and cons of the following types of media and instructional methods.

Media	Advantages	Disadvantages
1. Classroom instruction		
2. On-the-job training		
3. Books		
4. Video		

Media	Advantages	Disadvantages
5. **Simulation**		
6. **Practical workshop**		
7. **Text-based self-directed learning**		
8. **CBT Computer-based training**		
9. **IBT Internet- or Web-based training**		
10. **Multimedia**		

Media	Advantages	Disadvantages
11. The real thing		
12. Audio		

Any more? List them here, then compare your list with ours.

Answers

Media	Advantages	Disadvantages
1. Classroom instruction	Very flexible and economical. A skilled trainer can prepare a course very quickly and can cope with many different students. Can be interactive.	Variable quality, totally dependent on the skill of the trainer. Run at the pace of the trainer, not the trainee. Encourages a teacher - student dependency. May not be interactive.
2. On-the-job training	Can be best if the trainee gets gradual practice and feedback on real issues.	Totally dependent on the quality of supervision. Can be an excuse for doing nothing.
3. Books	Flexible, portable, economical, random access, allows note-taking, self-paced. Most students are familiar with use, permanent.	Depends on the study skills and motivation of the student. Essentially passive, with no mastery of objectives before a student can continue.
4. Video	Visual impact, shows movement. Can be used for large audiences. People like watching video. Can cover an enormous amount of information. Good at presenting a message with impact.	A passive medium over which the student has no control. No testing of understanding. Conveys enormous amounts of information. Can be too entertaining. Very expensive, involves many specific skills: script-writing, filming, audio, acting, etc.
5. Simulation	Allows practice and learning on something like the real thing, if the latter is too dangerous or expensive. Can be realistic and interesting. Involves interaction. Can be computer-based.	Expensive. Better to use the real thing if safety and cost not critical, e.g., software packages with training data.
6. Practical workshop	Allows interactivity. Can test the students' understanding by practical exercises. Allows discussion, questions and feedback. Cheap and flexible.	Dependent on the skill of the instructor. Good exercises take time to design. Can be difficult to run as students learn at different speeds.

Answers

Media	Advantages	Disadvantages
7. Text-based self-directed learning	Cheap, flexible, self-paced. Allows access at the students' 'pace and place'. All the advantages of books plus exercises to test understanding and interact with other media.	Depends on the quality of the design. Can be patronizing. Not fully interactive.
8. CBT Computer-based training	Consistent, cost-effective delivery to large audience. Can be interactive. Can involve testing to check understanding. Can manage other learning media and activities. Self-paced.	Needs large audiences to justify the cost. Totally dependent on the quality of the design.
9. IBT Internet- or Web-based training	Information and knowledge available just when you want it. Interactive, can send information and receive feedback. Instant updating of information and immediate feedback from users via e-mail.	Band width and slow delivery for interactive material
10. Multimedia	All the advantages of CBT, video plus sound, plus high-quality photographs and fast reference to enormous amounts of data through CD-ROM.	Just because it can do everything does not mean you need it. Very expensive.
11. The real thing	Very relevant, cheap.	People do not necessarily learn from experience and they may learn the wrong things.
12. Audio	Can simulate audio-based performance such as radio/ telephone techniques, languages. Cheap, portable. Student can control by switching off. Study on the move, e.g., in a car.	Generally passive. No note-taking. Learner's attention 'wanders' after a few minutes.

How did your list compare with ours?

The principal lessons are:

- Effective instruction often uses a mixture of media
- Use the strengths of one medium and compensate for the weaknesses in others
- Use the medium which is as close to the real thing as possible

Examples

A video	to get over a message and visual impact, e.g., selling the benefits of a training package
A workbook (text)	for the student to keep, refer to, and make notes on
Computer-based testing	to test a student's understanding before he or she progresses
Practical workshops	to allow practical experience, discussion, questions, feedback, etc.

Other influences on your choice will include:

- the learner's preference
- realistic constraints, e.g., cost and time
- what you are best equipped to use
- what would please the most people with the minimum effort

Remember:

The first principle of choosing a medium is to select the one which is as close to the real thing as you can possibly get. So if the performance involves interpreting forms with handwritten data then use example forms with handwritten data, ***not*** computer simulations of forms. If the performance involves operating equipment, your final objective will have to involve that equipment.

In designing a self-directed module, you are lucky because self-directed learning is an approach rather than a method, and a general term that covers many things, including multimedia, CBT, and workbooks.

Even a computer-aided lesson may have a workbook for reference and note-taking.

Finally ...

Using this book is not the best method for learning how to design effective self-directed learning. This is a skill that needs practice and feedback. You can learn the essential knowledge here but you will not become skilled until you have applied that knowledge and obtained feedback. That is why we recommend that you work with an experienced colleague or supervisor.

Now that you know something about different types of media, look at your pyramid again and check your grouping of topics into modules. Do they make sense in terms of things that can conveniently be learned together, e.g., similar methods, a skills workshop?

In our example we have added the units to the learning map because they include different types of learning which will need different media.

When you have done this for your pyramid, modify your learning map and annotate it with all the media to be used for each module or unit.

You can see from our example that a wide variety of methods are used and that you frequently have options. Real constraints will probably lead you to compromise, e.g., if you cannot afford video for module 4, and you are already using CBT for 3.2 and 5, you may well end up with a CBT simulation of 4. As long as it does not detract from the learner achieving the objectives, it will be easier for you to develop and may be easier for the learner to manage.

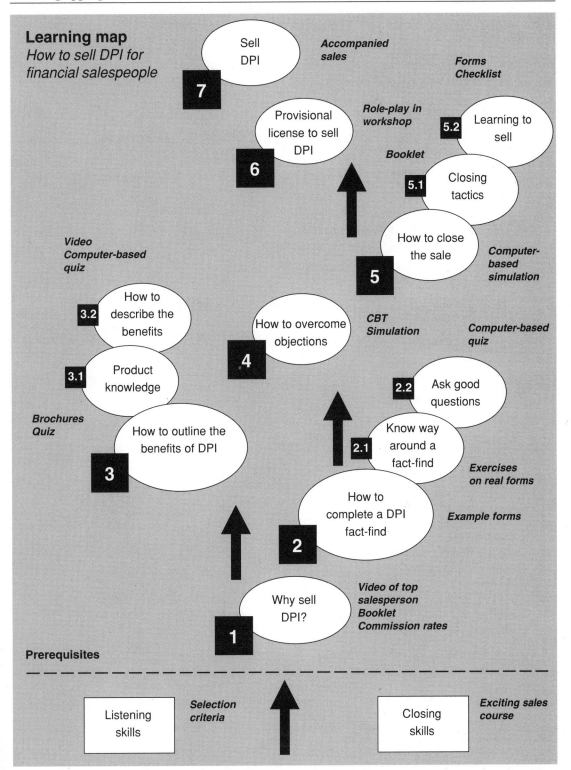

Learning map
How to sell DPI for financial salespeople

Sell DPI

Accompanied sales

7

Forms Checklist

Provisional license to sell DPI

Role-play in workshop

6

5.2 Learning to sell

Booklet

5.1 Closing tactics

How to close the sale

5

Computer-based simulation

Video Computer-based quiz

3.2 How to describe the benefits

How to overcome objections

CBT Simulation

4

Computer-based quiz

3.1 Product knowledge

2.2 Ask good questions

Brochures Quiz

How to outline the benefits of DPI

Know way around a fact-find

3

2.1

Exercises on real forms

How to complete a DPI fact-find

Example forms

2

Why sell DPI?

Video of top salesperson Booklet Commission rates

1

Prerequisites

Listening skills

Selection criteria

Closing skills

Exciting sales course

The final selection for our sales consultants

In this case we know that our target group wants to learn in short chunks and has multimedia. However, the final test of the training is probably best done as close to 'real life' as possible, so we would suggest:

1.   Self-directed learning package accessed via the company intranet

including workbook, video, computer-based quizzes, forms, product knowledge brochures.

2.   One-day role-play workshops

with video feedback and skilled salespeople

3.   Eight accompanied sales in six months with debrief

by manager before being awarded full license to sell DPI

Quiz

1. What are three of the four main reasons for use of performance aids?

> **1.**

> **2.**

> **3.**

2. From our list of advantages and disadvantages, name the following training medium?

Advantages

Can be best if the trainee gets
gradual practice and feedback on
real issues

Disadvantages

Totally dependent on the quality
of supervision. Can be an
excuse for doing nothing

Quiz

3. **Have you made a list of advantages and disadvantages of different types of media?**

No

Yes

Answers

---

1. What are three of the four main reasons for use of performance aids?

1.	**To jog memory**

2.	**To improve information**

3.	**To reduce complexity**

4.	**To identify something quickly**

2. From our list of advantages and disadvantages, what is the following training medium?

Advantages

Can be best if the trainee gets gradual practice and feedback on real issues

Disadvantages

Totally dependent on the quality of supervision. Can be an excuse for doing nothing

On-the-job training

Answers

3. **Have you made a list of advantages and disadvantages of different types of media?**

No   ➡   *Go on and do so now.*

Yes   ⬇   *This will help you choose the best mix of media for your projects.*

Unit 4

Starting the detailed design

Now you have broken down the topic into modules and units

- Where do you start?
- How do you give it some structure?

Objective

> *By the end of this unit you will be able to list the essential elements of a learning unit.*

Follow the steps in the unit and you will know that any module you design is well structured.

Quiz

1. **You have probably designed a lesson or a learning module before.**
    Assuming that you already have a design objective, what would you do next?

2. **How would you structure the module?**

Answers

1. **You have probably designed something before; a lesson or a learning module. Assuming that you already have a design objective, what would you do next?**

The next thing you do is to design the test or quiz.

When you have a measurable objective and an appropriate test, everything that you design to go in between must be relevant to both, or it doesn't go in!

This is the way to make your designs short and relevant

You do not start by research on writing content.

Keep away from those books!

2. **How would you structure the module?**

State the performance objectives
so that the learner can visualize himself or herself doing it

Sell the benefits
of doing it. You have a good idea of what motivates your students from your target group description

Check any prerequisites
so that people do not waste their time

Test existing competence

Offer learning activities for new skills and knowledge
or an option to take a test

Model the desired performance
give examples of the desired performance

Provide practice and feedback
make the exercises gradually more complex with decreasing help

Test that the learner can achieve the objective

Example of how to structure Module 1 'Why sell DPI?'

State the performance objective

Given the video and current commission rate booklet, make a commitment to complete the course, work out potential commission and benefits to you so that the commission test is +/- 5% accurate and you sign a commitment to training form

Sell the benefits

Video of top sales consultant describing benefits

Check any prerequisites

Check that the learner had achieved minimum sales of normal insurance in previous six months

Test existing competence

Quiz on questioning skills

Offer learning activities

Self-directed learning booklet and exercises on possible commission and benefits to you

Model the desired performance

List of top sales consultants who have already made a commitment

Provide practice and feedback

Not needed

Test

Quiz on commission. Training commitment form to be signed

Project activity

Think about your project. Choose an easy module or unit and draft out how you will structure it.

State the performance objective

Sell the benefits

Check any prerequisites

Test existing competence

Offer learning activities

Model the desired performance

Provide practice and feedback

Test

Quiz

1. **When starting to design a module, given the design objective what do you do next?**

2. **What are the essential elements of any learning unit?**

Answers

1. **When starting to design a module, given the design objective, what do you do next?**

> **Design the test**

2. **What are the elements of any learning unit?**

- **State the performance objectives**
- **Sell the benefits**
- **Check any prerequisites**
- **Test existing competence**
- **Offer learning activities for new skills and knowledge**
- **Model the desired performance**
- **Provide practice and feedback**
- **Test that the learner can achieve the objective**

Unit 5

Test question design

Any form of training needs to include plenty of questions to test the learners' understanding before they continue. This is particularly true of CBT, and other multimedia, when the computer needs to know what to show the learner next.

In designing good learning materials you will write lots of questions. This unit shows you how.

Objective

By the end of this unit you will be able to:

- *state the most important feature of any test question*
- *name the three ways that tests are used*
- *describe how to design a question*
- *name six rules for designing multiple-choice questions*

Introduction

A good interactive lesson needs questions because this is the way the student is asked to think about or do something.

Questions don't come out of thin air!

They come directly from the standard part of your design objective.

So, after you have written your objective, go ahead and design the questions that make up your test. This ensures that the content of your lesson is directly relevant to your objective.

Quiz
How much do you know already?

(An example of questions being used as a learning activity)

1. **What are the main ways that tests are used?**

2. **How do you design a question?**

Answers

1. What are the main ways that tests are used?

> 1. As a learning activity like this one
> 2. To check understanding
> 3. To test mastery

2. How do you design a question?

> Directly from the standards in your design objective

Lesson structure and question design

The most difficult questions to design are those that will be scored by computer. This is because they have to be so specific. There are four main question types used in CBT and multimedia:

- multiple choice
- alternative response (true/false)
- matching
- free form

Multiple-choice questions

These present a problem and a series of possible responses, e.g.:

Which of the following is a fruit?

a. potato ☐

b. raspberry ☐

c. carrot ☐   *(choose one option)*

The advantage of multiple-choice questions is that it is easy for the computer to match single key entries.

The disadvantage is that the questions are difficult to write well because suitable wrong choices (distractors) are often hard to find and the question gives many 'clues' to the student.

Alternative-response questions (true/false)

These give the learner a choice of only two responses.

They are fast to respond to and can reflect realistic occasions when learners are asked to judge a statement as being right or wrong.

They only cover small pieces of information and encourage people to guess.

Abraham Lincoln was the 16th President of the United States.

True ☐

or

False ☐   *(check the appropriate box)*

Matching questions

These present several 'premises' and possible 'responses.'

Match the following foreign bonds with their respective market of issue:

A. Samurais   United States_____
B. Matadors   Spain_____
C. Rembrandts   Portugal_____
D. Bulldogs   Belgium_____
E. Matildas   Japan_____
F. Navigators   United Kingdom_____
G. Yankees   Australia_____

A lot of information can be included without needing much testing time.

They are hard to design.

Free-form questions

Type in your answer

> ....

 Good for specific answers

 A very dangerous type, because it is hard to match all the possible right responses, especially in CBT, and there is a danger of giving inappropriate feedback.
It is best to use free format where there is only one answer. It is better if this is a number rather than a word, e.g., What is the melting point of steel?................°F

The six rules for designing multiple-choice questions

You have probably taken enough multiple-choice tests to have found ways of improving your chances.

Many questions give unintentional clues. There are six rules to follow to help avoid this:

1. Make sure the question tests the real performance
2. Present a clear problem
3. Use plausible choices
4. Avoid negatives in questions
5. Avoid 'none' or 'all' in questions
6. Avoid clues

Quiz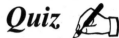

What is wrong with the following multiple-choice questions?

1. John Kennedy:

   a.   Served as ambassador to Britain during the Second World War
   b.   Served as the thirty-fifth president of the United States of America
   c.   Served as the national chairman of the United Fund campaign
   d.   Served as the president of the United States Senate

2. The increased speed was caused by an:

   a.   Additive
   b.   Faulty support
   c.   Small fitting
   d.   Stone

3. Which of the following is not an effective hangover cure?

   a.   Hanging upside down
   b.   Drinking a lot of water the night before
   c.   Aspirin
   d.   Hair of the dog

4. How many horses ran in the 1995 Kentucky Derby?

   a.   12
   b.   104
   c.   42
   d.   365

Answers

1. **This does not present a clear problem, and not enough of the item is included in the question.**

2. **A clue to the correct answer is given in the question; 'an' suggests that the correct answer is 'Additive.'**

3. **There is a negative in the question.**

4. **Not all the choices are plausible and it would be better to use ascending or descending numerical order.**

The seven rules for designing matching questions

There are seven rules for good design of matching questions:

1. Make sure it tests the real performance
2. Include clear directions for what the learner needs to do
3. Keep the items homogeneous
4. Make all the matches plausible
5. Offer more responses than premises
6. Keep responses shorter than premises
7. Use logical order

Some common errors

Directions: place the letter to the left of each number. Use each letter only once.

1. 91	a. **Engine with 12 cylinders**
2. Carburetor	b. **Mixes air with petroleum**
3. Spark plug	c. **Ignites fuel**
4. Windscreen	d. **Protects driver from wind**
5. V-12	e. **Measures engine size**
	f. **An octane rating**

These are premises   **These are responses**

What is wrong with the example?

- Each premise should relate to an engine part or a type of engine, but not to both
- Item 1 does not match feasibly with any alternatives except choice f
- Items are better arranged in numerical or alphabetical order

A better example

Directions: **Write the letter of the automobile part to the left of its function.**
              Not all the letters are used.

Function   **Automobile part**

1. **Mixes petroleum and air**	a. **Alternator**
2. **Assists in cooling**	b. **Carburetor**
3. **Protects driver from dirt particles**	c. **Radiator**
4. **Recharges battery**	d. **Spark plug**
	e. **Windscreen**

How are questions used in self-directed learning?

- To allow the learner to learn by discovery, e.g., by asking 'How much do you know already?'

- To test a learner's understanding before he or she progresses, e.g., by using a quiz.

- To test achievement of the standards for the objective, e.g., by using module tests or unit tests.

Remember!

People are often intimidated by tests, so use terms like 'quiz' or 'check yourself.'

Example

Test for Module 1 'Why sell DPI?'

The test questions always come from the objective:

Given	Module 1, video and booklet containing commission notes
Performance	Make a commitment to do the course to obtain a license to sell DPI, work out potential commission and benefits to you
Standard	Commission +/- 5% accurate
Method of assessment	Signed commitment

So appropriate questions are:

✓ / ✗

1. **Have you completed the exercise on identifying the benefits to you?**
   ☐

2. **Did you pass the commission quiz within +/- 5% of the correct answers?**
   ☐

3. **Have you signed the commitment form to do the course?**
   ☐

Practice

Take an objective from your unit and write a test question.

Show it to a colleague.

Does it meet the criteria on page 169?

Checklist

Does your test question:

✓

- **come from the standards in your design objective?**

☐

- **relate to the desired performance?**

☐

- **present a clear problem?**

☐

- **avoid unintentional clues?**

☐

- **test what you want it to test?**

☐

Quiz

1. What is the most important feature of any test question?

2. In what ways are tests used?

3. How do you design a test or question?

4. What are the six rules for designing multiple-choice questions?

| 1. |
| 2. |
| 3. |
| 4. |
| 5. |
| 6. |

Answers

1. **What is the most important feature of any test question?**

   > *That it is relevant to performance*

2. **In what ways are tests used?**

   > *1.   As a learning activity*
   > *2.   To test understanding*
   > *3.   To check mastery*

3. **How do you design a test or question?**

   > *Look at the standards part of your design objectives*

4. **What are the six rules for designing multiple-choice questions?**

   > *1.   Make sure the question tests the real performance*

   > *2.   Present a clear problem*

   > *3.   Use plausible choices*

   > *4.   Avoid negatives in questions*

   > *5.   Avoid 'none' or 'all' in questions*

   > *6.   Avoid unintentional clues, e.g., answers of a different length*

Module 3 Development

- ### *Unit 1*

Clear, effective writing

- ### *Unit 2*

Page design

- ### *Unit 3*

Screen design for CBT and multimedia

- ### *Unit 4*

Programmer-ready material

- ### *Unit 5*

Design for Web-based training

Unit 1

Clear, effective writing

Objective

> **By the end of this unit you will be able to:**
>
> - **name five guidelines for making your text readable**
> - **demonstrate six examples of poor writing that you have rewritten in an active, personal style**
> - **find a copy of suggested text standards**

Content is more important than presentation!

Page design cannot be considered in isolation. If your instructional design is poor, then no amount of effective presentation will make it effective. A key part of presentation is **clear, effective writing** that is appropriate to your target group. You have already seen that the more you can 'get into the shoes' of the target group, the better you can design effective materials.

Working with high performers and writing down what they say, in the way they say it, will also make your writing lively and appropriate. A key skill of design at this stage is how you write in the **active, personal style** rather than the passive, formal language often used by experts.

An example of passive formal language

Here is an extract from an English accounting textbook:

THE COMPANIES ACT

The accounting provisions introduced in the successive Companies Acts have not for the most part had the effect of forcing additional disclosures by most companies, but of bringing the minority of 'laggards' up to the standard of the majority.

The most basic effect of legal provisions is that accounts are publicly available for all companies. Every company must deliver a copy of its accounts to the Registrar of Companies for filing in publicly available files. The Companies Act 1976, sections 1-6, has tightened up the regulations for filing so that the accounts available in a company's files should no longer be out of date as they have been hitherto. In practice, public companies will always send a copy of their latest annual report and accounts to anyone who requests it.

You do not have to write like this.

If you take out the redundant information and use the active voice and personal style, you could present all the above information like this:

How to analyze other companies' accounts

Every public company must file a recent copy with the Registrar of Companies. Another good source is simply to phone the company concerned and ask for a copy.

If you are filing a copy, check the Companies Act 1976 (sections 1-6) for the regulations.

Which would you rather read?

Notice how all the same information is included in the second version.

Some guidelines for readability

- Write for your target group

- Use the active voice (subject, verb, object)

- Make it personal: 'You ...'

- Use short sentences

- Cut out redundant information

- Keep it concise!

- Link with graphics

- Get someone to criticize it

- Use headings to convey information actively, e.g., 'How to ...'

Quiz

Rewrite the following in a more active and interesting way.

1. **None of the above was understood by anyone.**

2. **Self-directed learning demonstration**

   This booklet that you are about to read consists of short extracts of self-directed learning produced for the MOG Fighter project. This project has been commissioned by the Borlandic Air Force to assist in the training of their pilots and weapon system operators.

3. **Busyness**

   One of the escape mechanisms from job-induced anxiety is the development of time-consuming activities that managers find less threatening to perform than the innovative or tough aspects of their job. This is labelled busyness.

Quiz

4. **Notice to all visitors**

   Will all visitors refrain from requesting to deposit luggage in reception.

5. *'This is the chief steward speaking. Will all passengers please note that the buffet car will be closing in 10 minutes. Will any passengers requiring refreshments during this time please come to the buffet car. The buffet is situated between first and coach class at the front of the train.'*

6. **This way to the fish shop.**

Answers

Rewrite the following in a more active and interesting way.

1. None of the above was understood by anyone.

> *No one understood it*

2. Self-directed learning demonstration

This booklet that you are about to read consists of short extracts of self-directed learning produced for the MOG Fighter project. This project has been commissioned by the Borlandic Air Force to assist in the training of their pilots and weapon system operators.

> *MOG Fighter Project - Self-Directed Learning Demonstration Booklet*

3. Busyness

One of the escape mechanisms from job-induced anxiety is the development of time-consuming activities that managers find less threatening to perform than the innovative or tough aspects of their job. This is labelled busyness.

> *Busyness*
>
> *One escape from job-induced anxiety is to do things that are less threatening than new or tough parts of a job.*

Answers

4. Notice to all visitors

Will all visitors refrain from requesting to deposit luggage in reception.

> **Sorry, we cannot keep your luggage in reception.**

5. 'This is the chief steward speaking. Will all passengers please note that the buffet car will be closing in 10 minutes. Will any passengers requiring refreshments during this time please come to the buffet car. The buffet is situated between first and coach class at the front of the train.'

'The buffet will be open for another 10 minutes.'

Performance aids showing direction to the buffet car

6. This way to the fish shop.

Unit 2

Page design

Objective

By the end of this unit you will be able to:

- *state five lessons of good page design for self-directed learning*
- *state the recommended minimum number of typefaces to use*
- *name four types of page in a skeleton lesson*

Exercise

Get hold of some self-directed learning materials.

- What layouts do you like?

- What layouts don't you like?

Here are some examples to get you started:

Example

Dolore: te feugait nulla facilisi. Nam liber tempor cum soluta nobis eleifend option congue nihil imperdiet doming id quod mazim placerat facer possim
Lorem: ipsum dolor sit amet, consectetuer adipiscing elit, sed diam nonummy nibh euismod tincidunt ut
Laoreet: dolore magna aliquam erat volutpat. Ut wisi

DELENIT AUGUE DUIS DOLORE TE FEUGAIT

Enim: ad minim veniam, quis nostrud exerci tation ullamcorper suscipit lobortis nisl ut aliquip ex ea
Vel: illum dolore eu feugiat nulla facilisis at vero eros et
Accumsan: et iusto odio dignissim qui blandit praesent luptatum zzril delenit augue duis dolore te feugait nulla facilisi. Lorem ipsum dolor sit amet, consectetuer adipiscing elit, sed diam nonummy nibh euismod
Tincidunt ut laoreet dolore magna aliquam erat.

Ut wisi enim ad minim veniam, quis nostrud exerci

Tation: ullamcorper suscipit lobortis nisl ut aliquip ex ea commodo consequat. Duis autem vel eum iriure dolor in hendrerit in vulputate velit esse molestie consequat,
Vel: illum dolore eu feugiat nulla facilisis at vero eros et
Accumsan: et iusto odio dignissim qui blandit praesent luptatum zzril delenit augue duis dolore te feugait nulla
Facilisi: Lorem ipsum dolor sit amet, consectetuer

ADIPISCING ELIT, SED DIAM

Nonummy: nibh euismod *tincidunt* ut laoreet dolore *magna* aliquam erat volutpat. Ut wisi *enim* ad minim
Veniam: quis nostrud exerci tation ullamcorper suscipit

Example

Et iusto odio

Lorem ipsum dolor sit amet, consectetuer adipiscing elit, sed diam nonummy nibh euismod tincidunt ut laoreet dolore magna.

- Aliquam erat volutpat

- Ut wisi enim ad minim

- laoreet dolore magna

Veniam, quis nostrud exerci tation lorem ipsum dolor sit amet, consectetuer adipiscing elit, sed diam nonummy nibh euismod tincidunt ut laoreet dolore magna

 luptatum zzril delenit augue duis dolore te feugait nulla facilisi. Lorem ipsum dolor sit amet, consectetuer adipiscing elit, sed diam nonummy nibh euismod duis dolore te feugait nulla facilisi.

Lorem ipsum iusto odio

Ullamcorper suscipit lobortis nisl ut aliquip ex ea commodo consequat. Duis autem vel eum

 Aliquam erat volutpat

 Ut wisi enim ad minim

Ex ea commodo consequat

Example

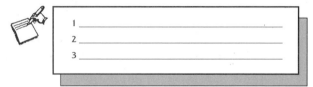

Incidunt 3

Dolore magna

Dignissim qui blandit praesent luptatum zzril delenit augue duis dolore te feugait nulla facilisi. Lorem ipsum dolor sit amet,

Consectetuer adipiscing elit, sed diam nonummy nibh euismod tincidunt ut laoreet

1 _____
2 _____
3 _____

aliquam erat volutpat.

-      ad minim veniam
-      quis nostrud exerci tation
-      ullamcorper suscipit

Ut wisi enim

lobortis nisl ut aliquip ex ea commodo consequat. Duis autem vel eum iriure dolor in hendrerit in vulputate velit esse molestie

consequat, vel illum dolore eu feugiat nulla facilisis at vero eros et accumsan et iusto odio dignissim qui blandit praesent luptatum

1 _____
2 _____
3 _____

Example

Lorem: ipsum dolor sit amet

Nobis eleifend option congue nihil imperdiet

① *Dolore:* te feugait nulla facilisi. Nam liber tempor

② Soluta nobis eleifend option congue nihil imperdiet doming id quod mazim placerat facer

③ *Lorem:* ipsum dolor sit amet, consectetuer adipiscing

④ *Enim:* ad·minim veniam, quis nostrud exerci tation

it amet,
consectetuer
adipiscing

am nmmy

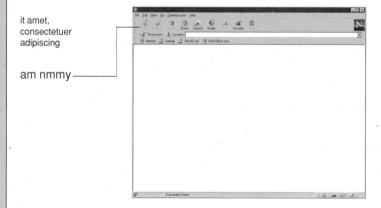

⑤ ***Accumsan:* et iusto odio dignissim qui blandit** luptatum zzril delenit augue duis dolore

⑥ **Te feugait nulla facilisi. Lorem ipsum sit amet,** consectetuer adipiscing

⑦ Elit, sed diam nonummy nibh euismod

⑧ Tincidunt ut laoreet dolore magna aliquam erat.

Example

Dolore: te feugait nulla facilisi

Nam liber tempor cum soluta nobis?

Bleifend option congue nihil imperdiet doming id
quod mazim placerat facer possim
Lorem: ipsum dolor sit amet, consectetuer
adipiscing elit, sed diam nonummy nibh euismod tincidunt
ut. *Laoreet:* dolore magna aliquam erat volutpat. Ut wisi
Enim: ad minim veniam, quis nostrud exerci tation
ullamcorper suscipit lobortis nisl ut aliquip ex ea
Vel: illum dolore eu feugiat nulla facilisis at vero eros et
Accumsan: et iusto odio dignissim qui blandit praesent
luptatum zzril delenit augue duis dolore te feugait nulla
facilisi. Lorem ipsum dolor sit amet, consectetuer
adipiscing elit, sed diam nonummy nibh euismod
Tincidunt ut laoreet dolore magna aliquam erat.

Ut wisi: enim ad minim veniam
Tation: ullamcoel eum iriure dolor in hendrerit in vulputate
velit esse molestie consequat,

```
Vel: illum dolore eu feugiat nulla facilisis at vero
eros et . Accumsan: et iusto odio dignissim qui
blandit praesent luptatum zzril delenit augue duis
```

Nonummy: nibh euismod tincidunt ut laoreet dolore

```
magna aliquam erat
volutpat. Ut wisi enim
ad minim
Veniam: quis nostrud
```

Commodo consequat. Duis autem vel eum iriure dolor in

```
Vel: illum dolore eu feugiat nulla facilisis at vero
eros et . Accumsan: et iusto odio dignissim qui
blandit praesent luptatum zzril delenit augue duis
dolore te feugait nulla
```

What did you think?

Good layout is very subjective.

Some of the things you may have noticed:

- Too much text can give a cramped feel to the page

- Just enough white space gives an active feel to the page

- Mix graphics, bullet points, and short sentences but don't overdo it

- Use unjustified right-hand margins (they are easier to read)

- Allocate areas of the page consistently for specific purposes

- Only use graphics for a purpose

- If you are using a binder, leave a wide enough inner margin

Typefaces

You will need help in designing a style sheet for your document. For a consistent look, choose two typefaces at the most, and decide when they will be used. For this book we have used:

Headline	Times Roman Bold 30 point
Subhead 1	Times Roman Bold Italic 22 point
Subhead 2	Times Roman Bold Italic 17 point
Subhead 3	Times Roman Bold Italic 14 point
Body text	Helvetica 9 point
Emphasis	Helvetica Bold italics

It is recommended that you get some help from a professional designer, choose typefaces and style sheets for your house style, and then stick to them.

A skeleton design

Each learning unit will have a similar structure.

You will have to decide on page layouts for:

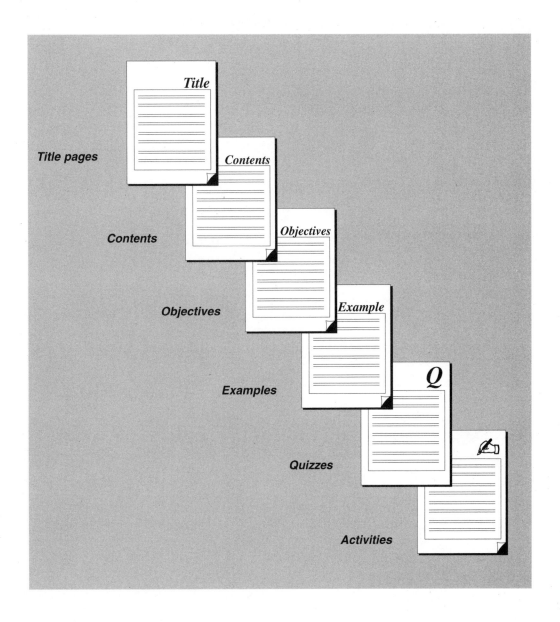

Some examples of how page layout gives the learner valuable information

Note:

1   how boxes and drop shadows always tell the reader that these are examples

2   how the action plan always has the same layout

3   how the gray backgrounds and white boxes are used when people have to fill something in

In this way the learner gets information without realizing it.

**Examples
of Vision Statements**

I.B.M.

'Our goal is simply stated.
We want to be the best

'We work with you to improve
people's performance in areas v
to the success of your business
We design and implement the be
training solutions so that you wa
to work with us again, and we ea
a reputation for doing the best w
in our field.

'Quality in all jobs - learn, th
analyze, evaluate and impr
Reliable products - on time,
excellence and consistency.
communication - listen, ask
speak up.'

'Budget Travel provides ecc
holiday travel and related s
to customers in the Londc
who expect efficient, probl
travel arrangements at low

Action	Who	Target
Date		

Read this unit, draft your
own Vision Statement

Get the CEO to decide whether
to produce a new Vision
Statement or modify
an existing one

Get the CEO to decide who
should be involved

Circulate this unit to the
team involved

Get them to record their i

Arrange a meeting to agr
Vision Statement

Find outside help if
necessary

Follow the format to agr
common Vision Statemen

Communicate the Vision
Statement to all staff

1

2

Vision Statement

To be completed by the top team.

What is the purpose of the organization; why does it exist?	
What products and/or services do you offer?	
What makes you distinctive from your competitors?	
What do you want to overhear your customers saying about you?	
What value will you offer to your customers?	
What value will you offer to your staff?	
Write a few short sentences to summarize the above. 'Our vision statement is that...'	

3

Testing and editing

Some desktop publishing tools are more difficult to use than word processors. You need an example of page layout to test with your target group, but the whole document does not have to be in this form. I recommend **producing the first complete module in finished DTP form but, if possible, leaving the rest in a good word processor.** Get your draft self-directed learning material checked and tested by a high performer/subject matter expert and by representatives from your target group. Keep the number of test copies to a minimum and ask people to make comments in different colored pens or on Post-it Notes which you can transfer to your master copy.

Do all this and edit as far as possible in the word processor before you give the material to your desktop publisher. You will save a great deal of time in producing your final document.

Quiz

1. State five lessons of good page design for self-directed learning.

2. What is the recommended number of typefaces to use?

3. Name four types of page that you might have in a skeleton design.

Answers

1. **State five lessons of good page design for self-directed learning.**

   - *Too much text can give a cramped feel to the page*
   - *Just enough white space gives an active feel to the page*
   - *Mix graphics, bullet points, and short sentences but don't overdo it*
   - *Use unjustified right-hand margins (they are easier to read)*
   - *Allocate areas of the page consistently for specific purposes*
   - *Only use graphics for a purpose*
   - *If you are using a binder, leave a big enough inner margin*

2. **What is the recommended number of typefaces to use?**

   Two

3. **Name four types of page that you might have in a skeleton design.**

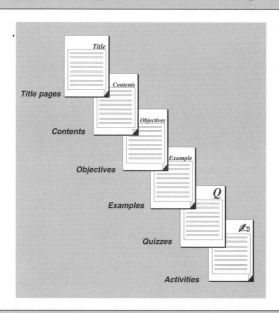

Unit 3

Screen design for CBT and multimedia

Objective

By the end of this unit you will be able to:

- state the key factors to be considered in screen design
- describe four general principles to aim for when using color on the screen
- describe the first secret of good screen design
- complete an exercise to redesign three screens
- describe how clear design objectives help you design multimedia or CBT

The key facts to consider

Screen design cannot be considered in isolation. If your instructional design is poor, then no amount of cosmetic presentation will save it from criticism.

The first factors to consider in any presentation are your *audience* and your *objective.*

A clear idea of the needs and constraints of your *target group* and what you expect it to be able to do (*the desired performance*) will allow you to cut out irrelevant material and present the key learning points as interactive activities, using language that means something to the learner, rather than the sort of language that generally appears in software manuals.

The active use of design objectives

How do we turn boring subject matter like the accounting text you saw earlier into an interesting screen-based unit?

Remember what it started off like?

THE COMPANIES ACT

The accounting provisions introduced in the successive Companies Acts have not for the most part had the effect of forcing additional disclosures by most companies, but of bringing the minority of 'laggards' up to the standard of the majority.

The most basic effect of legal provisions is that accounts are publicly available for all companies. Every company must deliver a copy of its accounts to the Registrar of Companies for filing in publicly available files. The Companies Act 1976, sections 1-6, has tightened up the regulations for filing so that the accounts available in a company's files should no longer be out of date as they have been hitherto. In practice public companies will always send a copy of their latest annual report and accounts to anyone who requests it.

To turn this into something more active we need to know:

• who the training is for

• what they need to be able to do with this knowledge

We can then write design objectives which will actually give us our screen design and test questions.

So the first secret of good screen design is to write good design objectives.

To find out our objectives we ask our high performer:

*   'Who are the people who use this knowledge?'

*   'What do they need to know in order to ...?'

Let's assume the first answer is

> **Trainee accountants**

The answer to the second question

What do they need to know?'

> **'the accounts are available for all public companies with the Registrar of Companies, or ask the company.**
>
> **You need to know the regulations for filing in the Companies Act 1976, sections 1-6.'**

This allows us to write three design objectives:

1. Given the need to analyze a company's accounts, state whether these are available to anyone.

2. Given the need to find a set of accounts, state two sources.

3. Given the need to check the regulations, state the year of the appropriate Companies Act.

We can then design three questions, add in a well, written summary for remedial feedback and an opening screen and we have the outline content to go on our screens. See page 209.

Screen content and flowchart

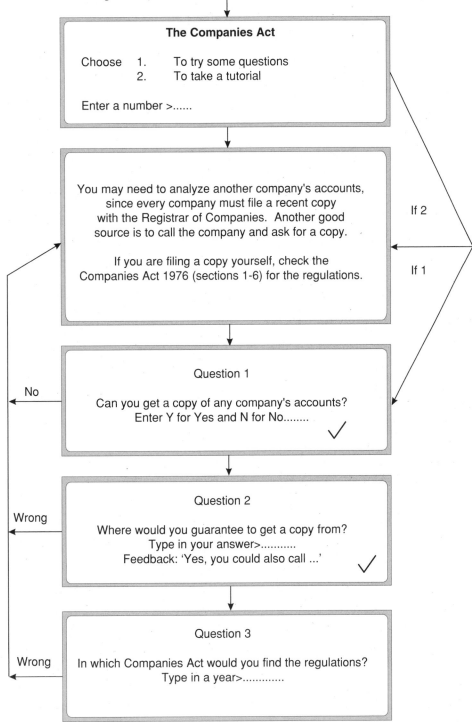

The Companies Act

Choose 1.   To try some questions
           2.   To take a tutorial

Enter a number >......

You may need to analyze another company's accounts,
since every company must file a recent copy
with the Registrar of Companies. Another good
source is to call the company and ask for a copy.

If you are filing a copy yourself, check the
Companies Act 1976 (sections 1-6) for the regulations.

If 2

If 1

Question 1

No

Can you get a copy of any company's accounts?
Enter Y for Yes and N for No........

Question 2

Wrong

Where would you guarantee to get a copy from?
Type in your answer>...........
Feedback: 'Yes, you could also call ...'

Question 3

Wrong

In which Companies Act would you find the regulations?
Type in a year>.............

Some presentation tips...

Contrast

A key principle of attractive design is smooth contrast drop, e.g., white lettering on a black background gives too much of a drop. A little theory ...

Black makes color and white appear more luminous.

White makes black appear more saturated and deeper.

Gray makes color appear more colorful.

Contrasting colors stand out from each other:

* *black and white*
* *black and yellow*
* *blue and white*
* *gray and white*

Brightness

Colors also vary in brightness according to the background with which they are contrasted:

So in your screen designs go for a stepped contrast drop, i.e., black border, blue or gray background and then white lettering rather than white on black. Try it on your computer and see what you prefer.

General principles in the use of color

Avoid:

- using colors for no particular purpose

- bright colors

- hot colors (e.g., pink and magenta appear to pulse on the screen; they are good for highlighting)

- too many colors

- noncomplementary colors e.g., red and yellow, green and blue

Aim for:

- consistent meanings for colors

- not more than four colors on the screen

- pale, pastel colors

- low-contrast background color, such as gray

- color contrast between character and background, e.g., white lettering on gray

- an overall style, e.g., with graded changes in contrast from background (gray?) to text (white) and highlights (red, yellow, green, pink).

Standard screen types

Just as with paper-based self-directed learning there are several types of screen that you will always need, e.g.:

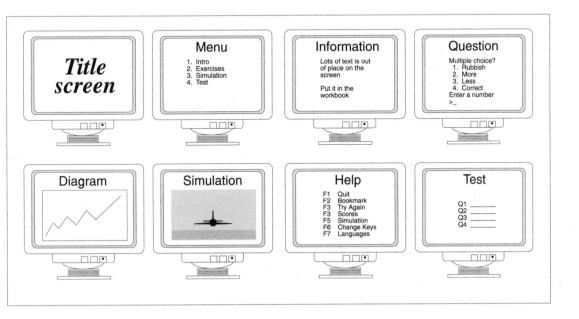

Why not produce skeleton designs for all of these?

This is especially important if you are designing as part of a large course and want to maintain a consistent 'identity.' A skeleton or standard lesson also acts as an extremely valuable performance aid for new designers.

Standard screen components

Reference information

The most common consideration for learners is 'How much is there still to do?' You can answer this by putting a module and unit name at the top of each screen and even a screen number. Use a consistent banner in a subdued color so that it blends into the border but the learner can find it if he or she wants to, just like the way *Windows* always tells you what file you are in.

If you are designing CBT for delivery via a Web browser such as Internet Explorer, you can use frames to segment off portions of the screen for use as a place marker or navigational aid for learners.

Function areas

It is a good idea to keep the screen components in function areas, e.g.:

Text and graphic areas

*   Avoid text which wraps around graphics.

Using frames in a browser allows for easy segregation. You may also consider providing thumbnail graphics which the learner can choose to bring to full size (or not) as needed.

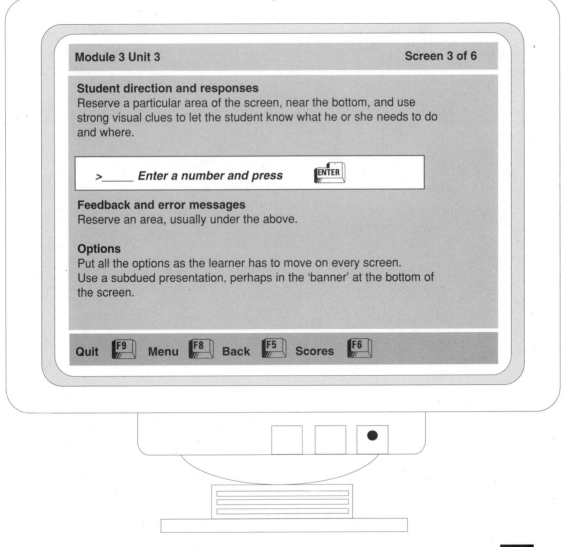

Module 3 Unit 3   **Screen 3 of 6**

Student direction and responses
Reserve a particular area of the screen, near the bottom, and use strong visual clues to let the student know what he or she needs to do and where.

> >_____ *Enter a number and press* **ENTER**

Feedback and error messages
Reserve an area, usually under the above.

Options
Put all the options as the learner has to move on every screen.
Use a subdued presentation, perhaps in the 'banner' at the bottom of the screen.

Quit F9   **Menu** F8   **Back** F5   **Scores** F6

Readability

You can see that the same rules about effective writing apply to text that appears on the screen but more so! People do not generally like reading from a screen. Basically, it is luminous, not reflective, and is harder to read.

A few guidelines for readable text on the screen

• Use as little text as possible

• Use short lines (like newspaper columns)

• Present text in natural blocks, not a page at a time (blank screens cost nothing, unlike paper)

• Do not indent

• Use ragged, right-hand justification, which is easier to read

• Avoid text wrapping around graphics

• Again, use as little text as possible (if there is a lot of text, put it in a workbook)

• Avoid too many fonts (no more than two)

Redesign the following real examples of screen design where little attention was given to the style of text or to the graphic power of the screen.

---

1. *If this is your first time using this style, it is recommended that you select the option 'Introduction to the system.'*

       1.   Introduction
       2.   Middle
       3.   Test

Make your selection by number or touch.

---

2. *BEACON DEMONSTRATION*

This demonstration shows the displays used to navigate a Cessna aircraft when it is being guided using a beacon.

The demonstration comprises a sequence of displays which indicate the position of the aircraft relative to the beacon, while approaching and landing on runway 5 at Kennedy International Airport.

You may stop the demonstration at any time by pressing the DATA key, and restart it by pressing the NEXT key.

Press the QUIT key to return to the menu.

Press the NEXT key to start the demonstration.

---

3. *COURSEWARE DEMONSTRATION*

The demonstration that you are about to see consists of a short sequence of courseware produced for the MOG project. The project has been commissioned by the Borlandic Air Force to assist in the training of their pilots and weapon system operators.

    Touch the screen or

    Press any key to continue

Redesign your screens here:

1

2

3

Answers

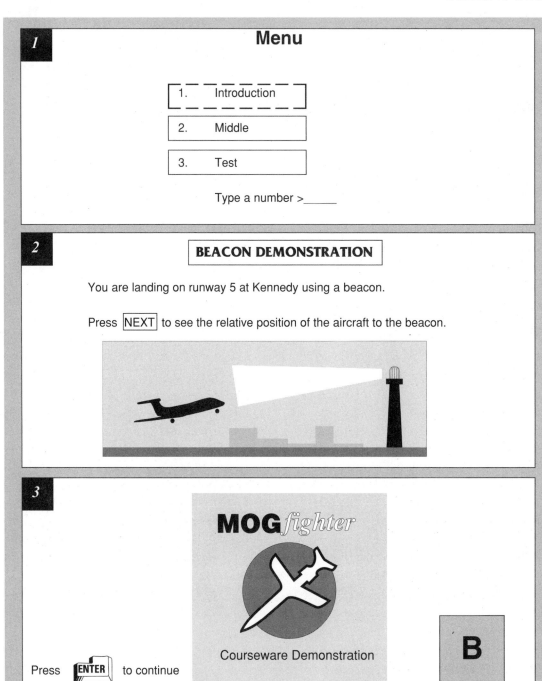

Computer-based simulation

This is often overlooked as a vehicle for self-directed learning but is a very effective method of learning.

One of our principles of good design is that the method you use should be as close to the real thing as possible. So what better than simulating the real performance?

Below is a simulation of how to spot hazards in an office which we designed for Scottish Widows.

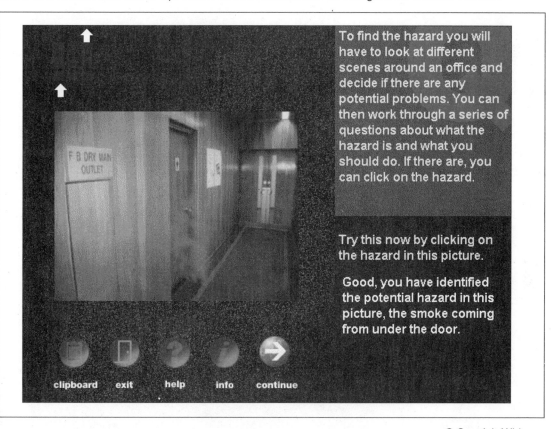

© *Scottish Widows*

The Learner walks through a virtual office, made of video clips, spotting potential hazards.

A computer-based situation simulation

In one example of a self-directed learning package, the design objective required the learner to spot opportunities for selling certain products during meetings with customers.

A prerequisite was a quick-reference product knowledge guide in the form of a small ring-binder showing all the products with their features and benefits.

We designed the following simulation to allow learners to:

- find which products best suited the customer's situation by trial and error in a series of simulated meetings

- test their product knowledge and ability to spot opportunities in a test versus the computer using a random set of simulations

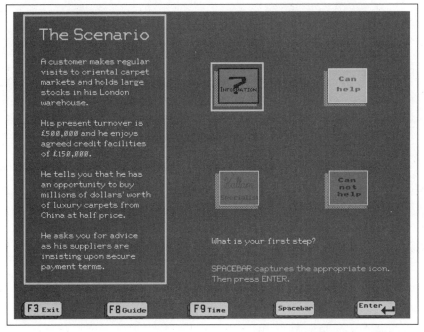

© *ACT Consultants Ltd.*

What is multimedia?

The screen below comes from a multimedia training package on how to use your phone.

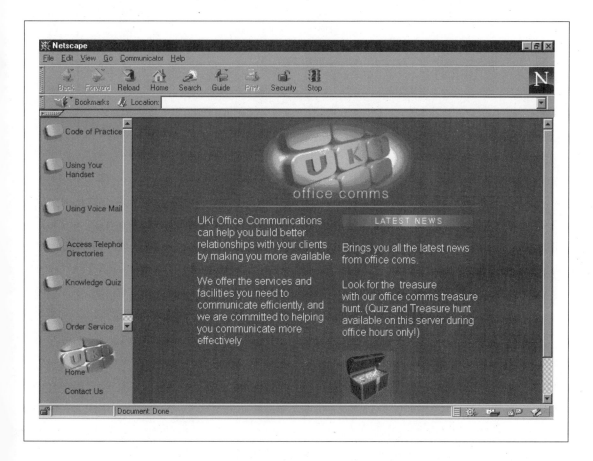

The buttons on the left take you to a Web site — telephone directory, clips of video, graphics, animation of – high-quality still photographs, a CBT quiz, and Internet-based phone directory.

Examples of multimedia

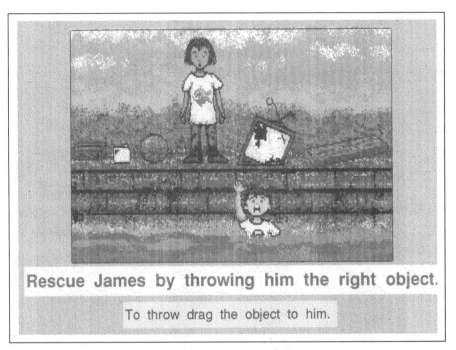

© CD Sports Ltd

Screen design for multimedia

One example of commercial multimedia has a garish brown menu screen with yellow lines all over it! The icons were colorful and novel and the whole thing looked a mess.

When we got into the lesson, the material was patronizing and educational. A tutor's voice told me what 'should happen.'

The text that appeared on the screen came straight out of a textbook and would scroll down as I read it.

Just because it is multimedia don't forget the principles of good design. They aren't new!

Whoever designed the multimedia above did not know:

- how to use color on screen (from CBT design)
- how to keep icons, routing and reference material unobtrusive (CBT design)
- that they could have used a *Windows*-based interface for an instant professional result
- how to focus on performance rather than knowledge
- how to rewrite text for the screen in an active, personal style

Multimedia is relatively new but the fundamental design skills needed to make it effective are not.

Good uses for multimedia

Multimedia can be used as an interactive and creative way to access information. For example, the *Musical Instruments* program allows learners to browse and discover in a very interactive way. You have all the advantages of an interactive book:

- high-quality illustrations
- flexible routing
- clips of sound
- video

It is no accident that the first effective examples of multimedia CDs were encyclopedias, and topics that need sound like music and language.

Another good use of multimedia is for language training...

...mainly because of the built-in sound facility that used to need a separate cassette player.
Now a microphone also allows you to record your responses and compare them with the pronunciation of the tutor.

Lots of good language-training materials already exist with booklets, audio and video tapes, and CBT quizzes which can now be brought together.

It can also enhance CBT.

The Mavis Beacon Typing tutor is a successful CBT lesson in its own right. This is because it is a performance-based package using the real medium of the keyboard to develop skills in a challenging and fun way.

The core design qualities have nothing to do with multimedia.

However, the multimedia version has better graphics and added sound feedback that makes it appear more attractive to the learner.

Beware of entertainment and attractive displays

There is a danger that multimedia, like CBT and (the now defunct) interactive video before it, will seduce people into thinking that just because something is more attractive, it must increase the motivation of the learner.

The cosmetic part of any package will soon wear off when the learner realizes that the material is not relevant and does not help him or her do things better.

Quiz

1. Write down the first two factors to be considered when designing a screen.

1.

2.

2. Describe four general principles to aim for when using color on the screen.

1.

2.

3.

4.

3. What is the first secret of good screen design?

Quiz

4. Have you completed the screen redesign exercise (page 218)?

✓

No

Yes

5. How do clear design objectives help you design effective multimedia training?

Answers

1. Write down the first two factors to be considered when designing a screen.

> **1.   The needs and constraints of your target group**
>
> **2.   The design objective**

2. Describe four general principles to aim for when using color on the screen.

> *Aim for:*
> - *consistent meanings for colors*
> - *not more than four colors on the screen (except graphics)*
> - *pale, pastel colors*
> - *low contrast background colors, such as gray*
> - *color-contrast between character and background, e.g., white lettering on gray*
> - *bright contrasting for diagrams and highlights, e.g., magenta or light green on gray*
> - *an overall style, e.g., with graded changes in contrast from background (gray?) to text (white) and highlights (red, yellow, green, pink)*

3. What is the first secret of good screen design?

> *To write good design objectives*

Answers

4. *Have you completed the screen redesign exercise (page 218)?*

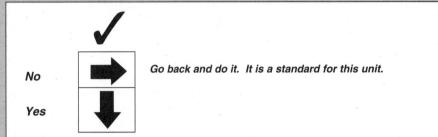

No

Yes

Go back and do it. It is a standard for this unit.

5. *How do clear design objectives help you design effective multimedia training?*

- *the conditions will tell you what scene to present on video, if necessary*
- *the performance tells you what the learner has to do, how he or she interacts with the computer*
- *the standards tell you how the learner, and the computer, know that the learner has mastered this bit and can move on*

Unit 4

Programmer-ready material

Objective

By the end of this unit you will be able to:

- *draw three standard flowchart symbols*
- *state what PRM stands for*
- *name the two main things included in a PRM binder*
- *describe five tips for writing clear PRM*

This unit has two sections:

- Flowcharting

- Programmer-ready material (PRM)

A CBT unit will probably have the following elements:

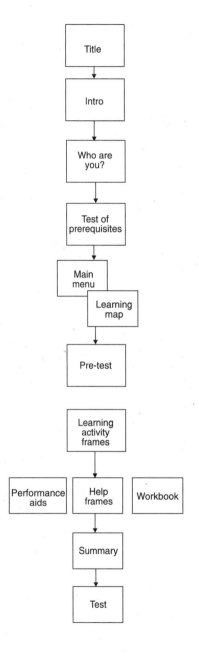

Use a representative graphic that embodies what the unit is about.

Outline the objectives and sell the benefits of the lesson, 'What it means to me.' 'What I will be able to do.'

State the target group and provide separate routes for other users, e.g., managers who want to browse through the material.

Test prerequisite knowledge, and don't let people continue until they pass.

Allow the learner to control his or her own learning from now on.

To see if the learner can master the objectives already.

Not teaching, but activities where the student can learn by discovery or doing in conjunction with a workbook and performance aids.

Reference information.

On-line help screens, possibly summarizing what is in the workbook.

Test to assess mastery of the objectives (the criterion test).

The diagram on the previous page is a simple flowchart.

We draw flowcharts for CBT and multimedia to check that:

* there are no loops
* all the responses are considered
* to let the programmer know where everything goes and how it links together

Start with an overview like the one on page 236, then produce more detailed flowcharts for the relevant elements.

Standard flowchart symbols

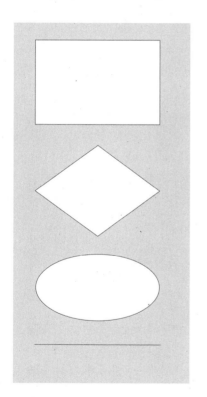

Represents information presented to the learner.

Represents routing decisions or shows that a response is needed.

Represents the beginning or end of a lesson.

Represents the direction of student flow through the lesson.

Note: Flow lines never cross.

Branching

Use the flowcharts to show the branching involved in your unit, depending on the learner's response, e.g.:

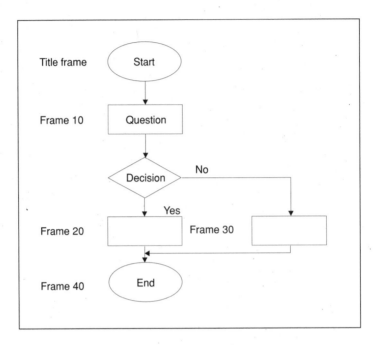

Label your frame numbers 10, 20, 30, etc., to allow room for additional frames, just like in programming.

How to draw a flowchart

- Make your flowchart fit on one page to make it easier to follow
- A box does not necessarily represent one screen
- If a sequence of screens is complex ,write a separate flowchart
- Put the following at the top left-hand corner of each page:
    - The page number. Your base flowchart should be No. 1
    - The coordinate for the left-hand axis of the matrix. This will always be a letter
    - The coordinate for the upper axis. This will always be a number

e.g.   1 B 1 refers to the symbol in B1 on page No. 1.

Flowchart

Module name:	Designer:
Demonstration First-level flowchart Sheet 1	Judith

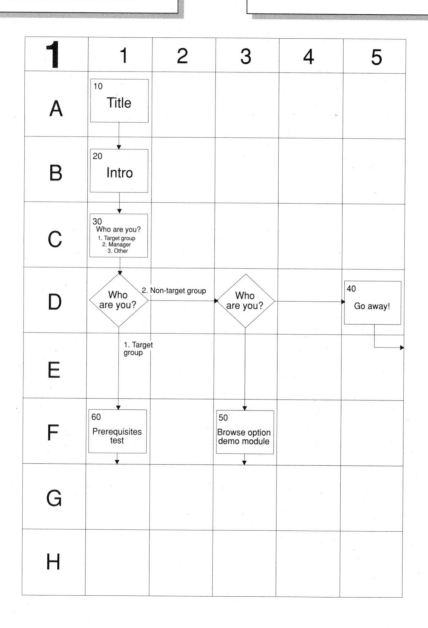

Flowchart

Module name:	Designer:
Demonstration	Judith
of 1 F 1	

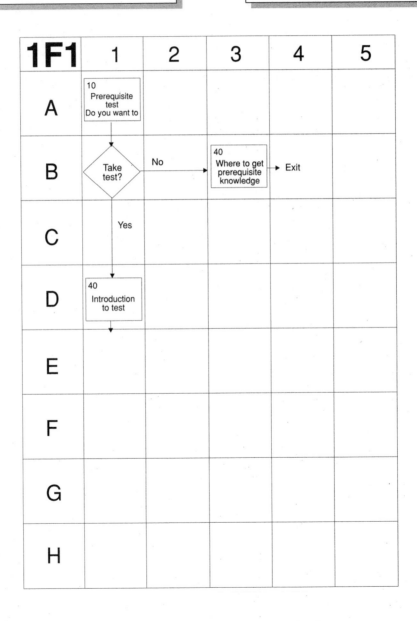

Don't be bound by convention

If traditional flowcharting does not work for you, then use your own variation.

In practice I use combined flowchart/screen design outlines, e.g.:

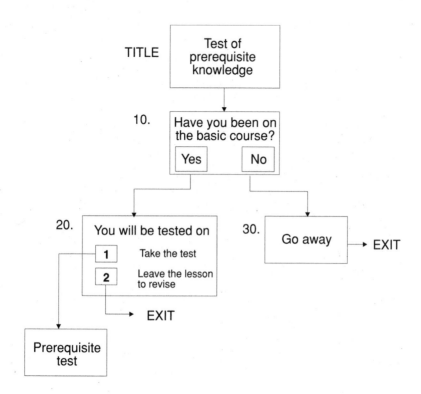

Draw a flowchart for any CBT part of your project.

Discuss it with a colleague. This is the main objective for this unit.

Programmer-ready material (PRM)

Now that you can design a flowchart you will need to pass the complete lesson design to your developer/ programmer. This is called programmer-ready material (PRM) and includes flowcharts and attached screen displays designed on screen design sheets.

An example of a simple CBT design sheet

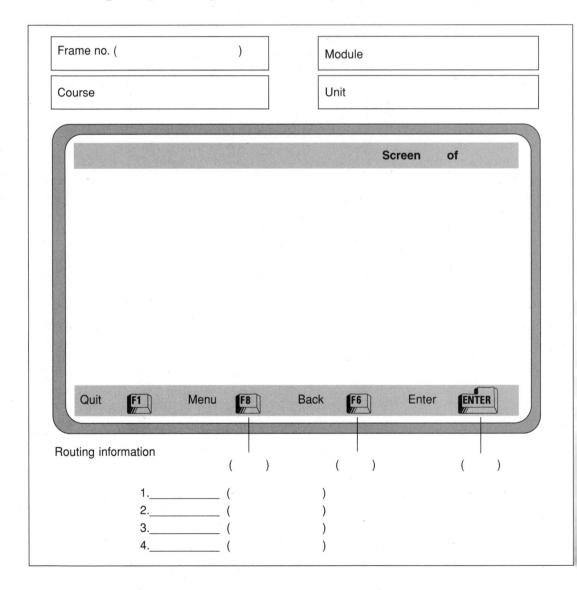

How much detail do you include in your PRM?

It depends on how confident you are in your programmer.

I prefer to give the basic information and leave issues such as color, text size, layout, etc., to his or her creativity, as long as the principles of good screen design are followed.

Some hints and tips about writing PRM

Do not use colored pens
The page may be photocopied!

Put the module name on every page
In case the pages get mixed up.

Number each screen
A good numbering system is 10, 20, 30, 40, etc. Later, if you need to add in a screen between 10 and 20 you can number it 15.

Eliminate text which has been crossed out
Your programmer may think that you want the student to see a crossed-out word! Use correction fluid.

Indicate where you want feedback to appear
In a consistent place.

State clearly which is the correct response to a question
It may not be obvious to the programmer.

Indicate how many times the learner can give a wrong response, e.g.:

He or she cannot move on until the correct answer is given.

If the learner answers wrong twice, give the right answer before moving on.

First time wrong	_____	feedback is 'no, try again'
Second time wrong	_____	feedback is a hint
Third time wrong	_____	feedback is the correct answer

To store the learner's response for later use
Indicate on the screen where you collect the response and state where it will be used.

For each test state the standard of mastery
You may want the learner to go back to the previous section if his or her performance is below a certain level.

Use your screen numbers to indicate the route(s) from each display, e.g.:

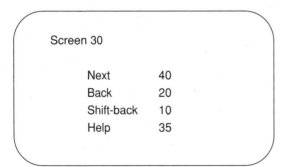

```
Screen 30

        Next        40
        Back        20
        Shift-back   10
        Help        35
```

If a screen is repeated
Give the frame number where it is to be used again.

Bind the PRM together with the flowchart
So that it cannot get mixed up.

Design for multimedia

You can design a multimedia lesson using very simple and accessible software, e.g. *Toolbook.*

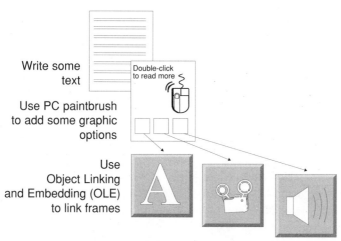

Write some text

Use PC paintbrush to add some graphic options

Use Object Linking and Embedding (OLE) to link frames

You will need a combined screen design/flowchart similar to CBT but with more options.

Structure

You need a mental picture of the structure of your program. This will probably look hierarchical when you draw it but it can still be totally flexible for the learner. Put this at the front of your flowcharts. Your challenge as a designer is to help learners keep a clear picture in their heads of the course structure, while still allowing them the freedom to roam around it, e.g.:

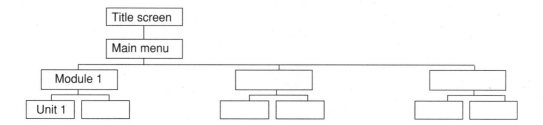

Beware multimedia teaching!

Voice instructions, high-quality photographs, and hypertext that allows 'hot links' make multimedia a very seductive teaching machine. The danger is that it may be used in this way to teach or tell the student via the PC.

Multimedia is also very good at giving access to vast amounts of information, both in visual and text form. However, we have seen that good instructional design involves reducing the amount of knowledge a learner needs to a minimum. There is a danger that multimedia could encourage the sort of educational, knowledge-intensive training that self-directed learning has been breaking down.

Multimedia is not the answer on its own

It is excellent for interactive access to vast amounts of information.

Training programs with specific objectives often use multimedia reference banks to allow students to learn by discovery. For example, high school music classes may quiz students to find certain information. The students then use the *Musical Instruments* CD to find the relevant information for their course. We may find training programs dipping into generic CDs or Web sites as part of their courses.

Good learning materials should always involve a mix of media

Even with multimedia, learners will want workbooks to take away and hard-copy quick-reference guides to use at short notice.

Multimedia is not the ultimate self-directed learning delivery method but one of several options you should consider

Good design for multimedia is the same as for all other methods. The *CDI Designers Guide* (McGraw-Hill, 1993) says of instructional design: 'Any of the fundamental principles of instructional design are relevant in any platform, whether the end product be a children's game, an electronic brochure, or a training package.'

This book is about the fundamental instructional design you will need to make your multimedia objective. This is no different from any other method.

Quiz

1. **Draw the standard flowchart symbols for the following:**

   a. **Information**

   b. **Decision**

   c. **End of lesson**

2. **What does PRM stand for?**

3. **Give five tips for writing clear PRM.**

   1.

   2.

   3.

   4.

   5.

Answers

1. Draw the standard flowchart symbols for the following:

   a.   **Information**

   b.   **Decision**

   c.   **End of lesson**

2. What does PRM stand for?

> Programmer-ready material

3. Give five tips for writing clear PRM

1.	Do not use colored pens
2.	Lesson name on every page
3.	Number each frame
4.	For complex displays, draw individual components, then the final screen
5.	Use correction fluid, don't cross out unwanted text
6.	Indicate where feedback should appear
7.	State your short correct and incorrect feedback
8.	State the correct response clearly
9.	Indicate how many times the student can give a wrong response
10.	Indicate where you want to collect responses
11.	State conditions for mastery of tests
12.	Put routing on each screen on the flowchart
13.	Indicate repeated frames
14.	Bind it!

Unit 5

Design for Web-based training

Objective

> **Prerequisite:** *Before reading this unit, read the previous three units on effective writing, page design, and screen design for CBT and Multimedia*
>
> *By the end of this unit you will be able to:*
>
> *describe what WBT, WBL, and IBT are*
> *describe how WBT can be used to manage learning*
> *state the key factors to be considered in Web-based screen design*
> *find examples of Web page design*
> *find an exercise on screen design and examples*
> *find a list of recommended Web sites to visit*
> *name the new things that WBT allows us to do*
> *find a list of useful references*

Acknowledgment and thanks

I must admit that when I came to write this module I had never designed any WBT. Having said this, I know that it is just another delivery mechanism and that the fundamental principles would be the same as for CBT and any medium. I set out to find out what was different. To do this I asked the most experienced people I knew "What was different?" I asked Dave Cook who is a hugely experienced training consultant with Reuters and has designed and managed much of their use of WBT in the U.K. I asked Jenny Hayes who is a talented author and WBT designer. I also received help from my colleague Tim Ray who runs seminars on the use and potential of intranets for delivering learning. What follows is my interpretation of their experience. Many thanks for everyone's help.

This module is a little different from the others. Use the Web page opposite to navigate your way around.

Most of the principles of design are the same as for other methods of delivery, so you may have to look elsewhere in the book,

see page 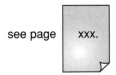 xxx.

You should also look at some real Web sites. We have given you some examples to get you started.

Have a look at our Web site at:

http://www.actconsult.co.uk.

Have fun!

Contents

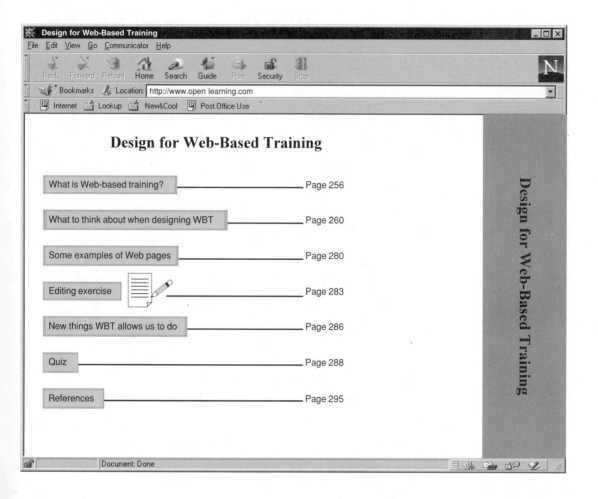

Design for Web-Based Training

What is Web-based training?

Web-based training (WBT) is loosely used to describe any learning or training delivered over the Internet or an intranet within an organization.

To be pedantic, we could say that WBT contains the same elements as CBT. So just as CBT is made up of computer-aided learning and computer-managed learning, WBT is made up of:

> *Web-based learning and Web-managed learning*

Web-based training is fundamentally another delivery mechanism for training and learning and...

As such the same fundamental principles of screen design apply as for CBT and multimedia. However, WBT is more than another delivery system because it allows two-way communication which makes it more powerful than CBT or multimedia because it can allow:

- *access to information*
  - *company data via the intranet (continually updated)*
  - *global sources of information via the Internet*
- *on-line discussion*
  - *with trainer*
  - *with fellow students/learners*
  - *with other interested parties (including 'experts')*
- *structured interaction*
  - *trainers can collect data on learners' progress*
  - *trainers can assess learners' performances*
  - *trainers can give feedback*
- *on-line testing*
  - *trainers can test courseware*
  - *learners can do quizzes/simulations, etc., to test own performance (can be automatically assessed)*
- *on-line booking of learning and training activities*

The Web is especially good at allowing learners to assess their own needs via interactive needs analysis tools and then to find appropriate learning resources via access to external and internal database of resources. See the example of an interactive **learning map** on Reuters U.K. Training Web site. Clicking on any module leads to the learning materials.

An Interactive Learning Map

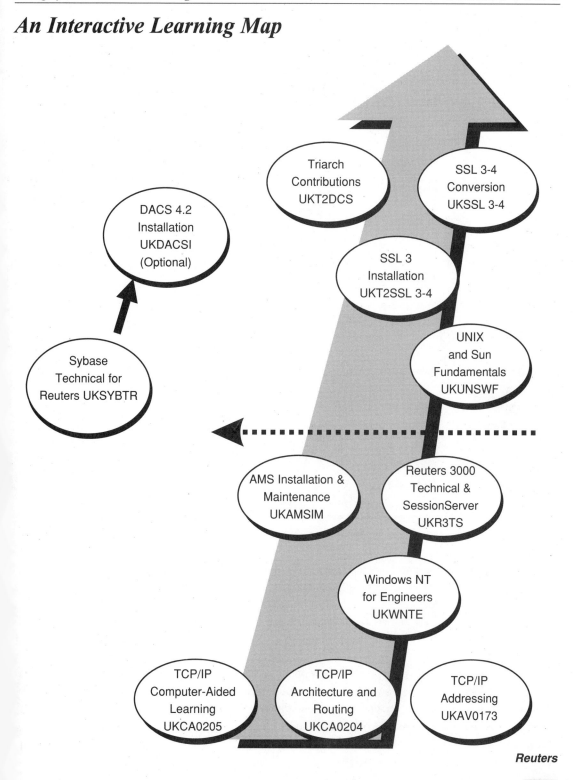

Triarch
Contributions
UKT2DCS

SSL 3-4
Conversion
UKSSL 3-4

DACS 4.2
Installation
UKDACSI
(Optional)

SSL 3
Installation
UKT2SSL 3-4

UNIX
and Sun
Fundamentals
UKUNSWF

Sybase
Technical for
Reuters UKSYBTR

AMS Installation &
Maintenance
UKAMSIM

Reuters 3000
Technical &
SessionServer
UKR3TS

Windows NT
for Engineers
UKWNTE

TCP/IP
Computer-Aided
Learning
UKCA0205

TCP/IP
Architecture and
Routing
UKCA0204

TCP/IP
Addressing
UKAV0173

Reuters

So WBT can be used to manage learning?

To replace traditional training information and course booking:

- To browse a list of training solutions
- Study role-specific learning maps
- Make on-line booking of self-directed learning materials and training
- Downloading of learning materials

It can also offer:

- Interactive needs analysis
- Testing
- Tutorials
- Conferences, etc.

Frequently used terms

Just like other new technologies, the Web has spawned its own jargon words. Here are explanations of just a few of the more commonly used technical terms to help you understand the basics.

Browsers are the software packages that allow computers to communicate information between separate devices. They help to overcome the problem of machine incompatibility that used to prevent different types of computers talking to each other and accessing each other's files. They can only read certain sorts of files (e.g., HTML and JAVA files). The two most popular browsers are Netscape Navigator and Internet Explorer.

Frames are a way of dividing pages into window panes or 'frames.' This format of page is only supported by the more recent versions of browsers. The page looks divided and each part or frame can be accessed independently — but clicking a link in one frame may replace the page in another frame in the same set. This is useful if you want to display some information like an index or contents listing for a site at all times while being able to change other information.

JAVA is a platform-independent programming language developed for the Web by Sun which is particularly useful for transactional processing (i.e., where the Web page needs to send information back to the server).

HTML is the mark-up language that allows all the browsers running on different computers to access and display the information held on the page. There are several software packages (such as Microsoft's FrontPage and Adobe's PageMill) that automate the marking up of pages in HTML. These packages allow you to preview pages, view them in layout mode, and also examine and change the underlying HTML coding.

Shockwave files are highly compressed multimedia movies. They are produced using Macromedia Director and can compact files sufficiently to be able to convey some animations, sound, and video quickly over the Web. You need to have the Shockwave plug-in in your browser to be able to view Shockwave movies. Shockwave is a very useful tool if you wish to show animations on your Web site.

However it is also possible to define simple animations as **GIFs** which can be viewed without the Shockwave plug-in. There are shareware packages like Gifbuilder, which automate the creation of these animations.

Links in the text of a page are simply the addresses of other pages on the Web. By clicking on them to make them active, you tell your browser to go find the address given by the code associated with the link. These addresses are often called **URLs** (Uniform Resource Locators).

Bandwidth is particularly a constraint on the design of Web sites that will be accessed via the Internet. It is the limitation of speed at which information can transmit across the network and into the user's computer. It is not such an important issue for Web sites that will be accessed over corporate intranets (although video with sound can still be rather demanding on network capabilities).

What to think about when designing WBT

Fundamentals

The first thing about design for WBT is that the fundamentals are no different from any other type of learning materials. You still need to be clear about:

> *Who it is for*
> *What the performance gap is*
> *The performance that you want to see*
> *The learning objective*
> *The knowledge and skills to meet this (pyramid analysis)*
> *Good screen design principles, use of color, layout, etc.*

So... if you are not clear about any of these things, go back and look at them now.

Ready now?

What is different about Web sites that I need to consider in design?

Three main things:

> *The two-way communication*
> *Hyperlinking*
> *Multimedia*

The two components of Web design are:

> *A usable structure*
> *The 'look and feel' of the pages*

How to design a usable Web site

If you are familiar with Web sites you may think that the beauty of on-line information is that it doesn't have any real structure because everything is available through the links between pages. But actually it takes a good underlying design to ensure that all the information you want is at your fingertips, or just a link away. If you place information higgledy piggledy onto a bunch of Web pages with lots of links between each page, you simply end up with a morass of information and no clear sense of how to find out what you need to know.

You need to plan your Web sites carefully. The information needs to be grouped into appropriate categories so that it can be found when required. Use the pyramid analysis that you learned in Unit 2 of Module 2 as a good method of grouping the contents of a Web site. You can generate a pyramid of 'Web pages' and keep adding or moving the Post-it Notes until you feel happy with the overall structure. Once you've done that, you can draw it out and start to add the links between pages as you work out how people will need to navigate through the site.

Use a large sheet of paper for your plan as the links can make it look very messy. You may want to draw primary links (the routes you want people to follow) in one color and secondary routes (perhaps to reference material) in another color. Write up any 'common' links as notes at the bottom of your plan (e.g., all pages may be linked to the home page and to the e-mail form).

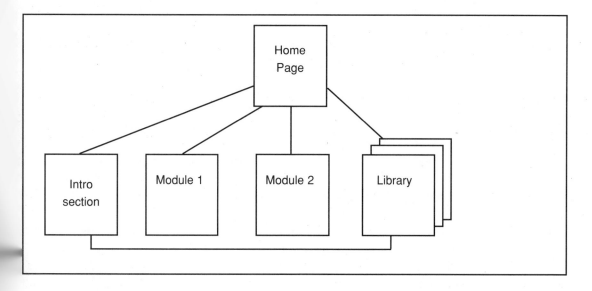

On larger sites, use some pages as 'contents pages' and provide the intermediate links between related pages and groups of pages. If your browser supports 'frames' (a way of dividing up the page into several windows) then you will be able to keep a site map or index on-screen permanently and this can be a big help in keeping the user oriented.

Because Web sites can contain hundreds or even thousands of pages of information, it is vital that you define a navigation metaphor that will help the user to keep track of where they currently are and to find where they want to go. Common metaphors for organizing information on the Web include maps, filing cabinets, buildings, books, and indexes. (See p268 for a good example of the file-tab metaphor in use.)

The metaphor you choose will help to define the 'look and feel' of your site.

If you have a lot of pages, you simply cannot link every page to every other page, as this would be utterly confusing to the user.

It's worth remembering that you can also have links within pages, so that you can create what is effectively a very long page, but that has links between its different components so that the user can jump to the section that interests them, while still being able to instantly access the material around it.

Or you can create many short pages (which saves the user from endless scrolling) and link them to each other.

Sales Training
Presentations skills
Negotiation skills
Questioning
Objection handling

Presentation skills

Confidence lies at the heart
of an effective presentation.
If you feel you know your
subject and your audience's
interests then you will have
the confidence to present
your information in a
convincing way, because

One useful question to ask yourself is:

How far do you want to control the passage of the user through your site?

For example, if you are devising a site to offer learning resources on an ad hoc basis, you probably don't want a strongly structured site, but you do want to make things easy to find. In this instance, indexing or search facilities are going to be at the top of your priority list. If, on the other hand, you are creating a site that features a number of on-line tutorials that people must work their way through in a specific order, then you will want to control their passage through the site, so that they follow your learning plan and this will mean limiting their access to various pages.

What does this mean in reality?

Imagine the example of a new front-line customer service representative who will be taking customer orders over the phone. You may want to ensure that this person achieves competency in three aspects of work before being allowed to deal with any external customers. These three areas might be 'basic company knowledge,' 'the phone code,' and 'taking orders.' So you might create three sets of Web pages covering the learning objectives for these subjects:

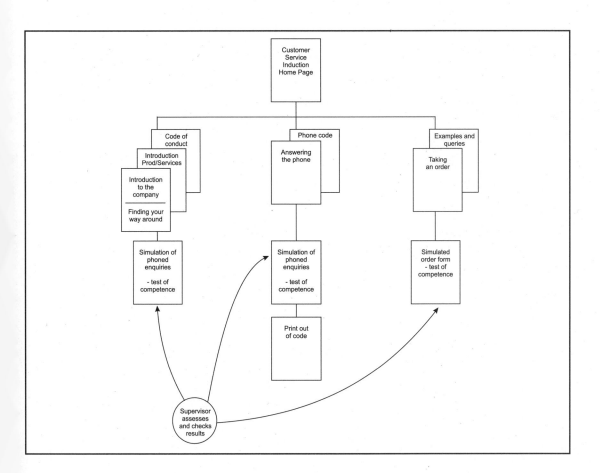

But you may also be asked to put a performance aid on your Web site to cover the needs of service engineers who are out at customers' sites and sometimes need detailed technical information to help them fix equipment. In such a case, you may want the customer service engineer to be able to quickly access the 'technical help points' and pick out the relevant help page. In which case, the structure might be quite different:

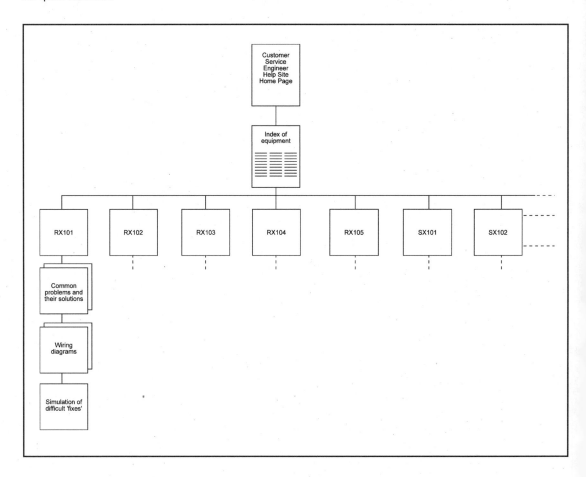

The last two examples looked at the extremes of structured versus open access to the resources on your Web site, but it is also possible to think of examples in the middle. Consider a group of supervisors who want to advance their professional competence. Each supervisor might have an individual development plan held on the Web site that would help to direct them through the relevant learning modules (structured access), but they may also want to investigate learning resources as problems arose in their work (ad hoc access). In such circumstances, you would need to modify and increase the links between pages for a structured approach that supported investigative forays:

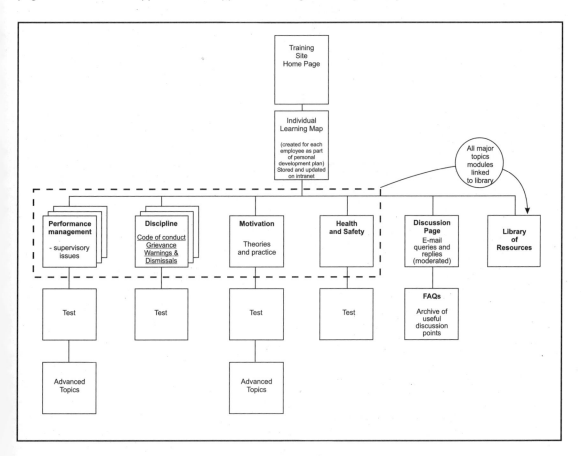

Each of the above designs is individually tailored to the needs of the target group that will use it, but sometimes it is more difficult to anticipate or define the needs of the target group for a Web site. For example, imagine that you have been asked to put all your organization's distance learning materials onto the intranet in a way that people can access them, as they needed them. The way to tackle this might be to create a 'virtual' training center and use a classroom-based metaphor to help people navigate around the site.

If you create a site that contains a lot of material — hundreds or thousands of pages of text and pictures plus video footage and multimedia packages — then you will need to index it carefully so that people can easily find what they require. (And so that you can easily maintain and update it.) Use a simple 'search engine' as the front end so that people can type in keywords to find links to useful material. Or if you don't have the resources or access to the expertise necessary to create a searchable database, create an index, or even an index of indexes that the user can access to find their needs.

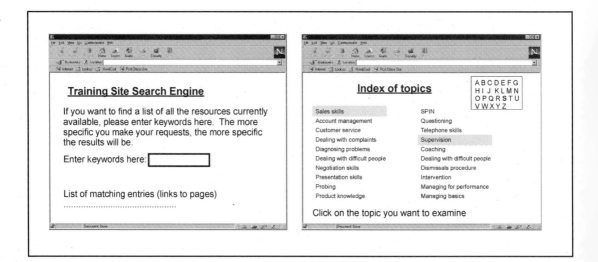

One other reason that structure is so important...

Structure is important not just to your site users but also to the person responsible for maintaining and updating your Web site (it might even be you!). If you don't have a clear plan of your Web site from the beginning, it can be very hard to implement changes that keep your Web site topical and properly cross-linked. Web site maintenance can become a major burden if it isn't planned for at the beginning.

New facilities we can use

Forums

Forums allow the learner to share problems and discuss solutions using moderated chat rooms if the learners are on-line at the same time.

Conferences

Learners are not on-line at the same time, but can use e-mail to communicate messages to a whole group. Messages and replies are posted to everyone within the designated learning group.

Learner choice

Hyperlinking allows learners to control their learning and skip about at will. This can be an advantage and a disadvantage. You can get just what you want or you can get hopelessly lost. Careful use of hyperlinks is a key design consideration. The learner must know that they have mastered what they need to before they move on so good test design is essential, just like any other media.

Attractiveness

Sometimes confused with motivation. The use of sound, pictures, color, etc., can enhance a unit if used for a purpose but can also turn it into 'entertrainment'. Again, use enough to help achieve the learning objective, no more.

Encourages exploration

Web sites can be tremendously supportive of investigative learning: the self-motivated learner can explore more widely and more easily than with traditional types of learning material.

An example of a file tab metaphor

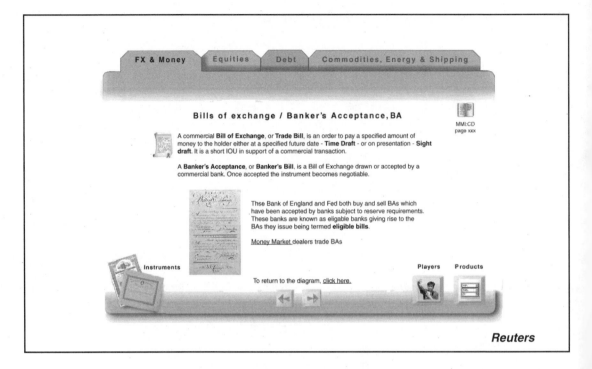

This Web site uses file tabs as a graphical device to help users find their way around. The visual metaphor of the file tab is one which everyone recognizes. Users can see all the main section headings, identify which section they are currently in, and jump easily between sections without getting lost.

Think Ahead

Have a structure in mind that can cope with adding pages and links. You are sure to do it, as one of the great attractions of Web sites is that they are so easy to extend and update. One of the great advantages of Web sites is that they can be very topical and communicate the very latest information. This means that you do need to build in a maintenance budget and method of tracking and evaluating use so that the site can be continuously improved and updated.

Some traps and how to avoid them

Getting lost

It seems to me that one of the greatest dangers of WBT is getting lost.

Hints

Just as in CBT design, always give the learner some reference point so they know where they are as well as choice to move about to other units. Designers use a number of interface metaphors, books, buildings, desks, etc. The file tab idea opposite is very common and works well. On-screen, site 'maps' are also good ways of giving the user a clear sense of where they are.

Feeling out of control

Interactivity is one of the key benefits of WBT, so it is vital that the user has control over the delivery of information and knows how to use it.

Hints

The learner should always feel in control. Learning should be an empowering experience not a confusing one. Just as in CBT design, make sure that you avoid timed presentations. Everyone reads and learns at their own pace (unless you are in a classroom!). Make sure that people understand your video and audio sequences and give them the option to ask for help or see/hear them again.

Make it easy for the user to stop at any point in the site and 'bookmark' their position so that they can return to it easily. This will enable them to step in and out of the site without wasting time scrolling through pages searching for where they got up to last time. The main browsers support bookmarking, but sometimes users need to be reminded to carry out this activity and you need to make sure that your Web pages are tagged with meaningful names, so that the bookmark is self-explanatory.

Be wary of large graphics and streaming audio and video. They can appear very slowly to the learner. Check on the capabilities of your network and delivery infrastructure. If in doubt keep it simple. Put in some text or a very simple graphic at the top of the page so that the learner has something to look at whilst a larger picture builds up.

Some advantages and how to exploit them

Inevitably some of the features on WBT that lead to traps also lead to the most attractive features.

Interactivity

Just like well designed CBT, you can use the interactive power of the Web to challenge the learner to learn by experience, to try things out. Make sure you explain what is happening at all times, give responses to all clicks, and let them return to a safe tutorial if they get stuck.

Topicality

The biggest advantage that WBT has over other media is that it can be totally up to date for all users. A procedure or policy on a company intranet is the correct version, now! You can also instantly change learning materials to reflect changes in policy, law, procedure and to reflect new ideas, feedback from users, etc. This is a tremendous advantage in our fast-moving world.

Feedback

Unlike CBT, WBT allows proper feedback. You can build e-mail into any or all your Web pages. A learner can send their comments to your feedback address simply by clicking the mouse button twice and typing in their comments. They can offer useful tips and ask questions for others to answer in an on-line discussion group. To do this, make sure that it is easy for your learners to comment and query your material and give them permission to do so. This means including feedback e-mail forms and creating a discussion page (with a moderator) and publishing common questions and answers.

Pictures and animated diagrams

Bearing in mind the dangers of slow download speed mentioned earlier, you can show high-quality pictures and photographs and animated diagrams to illustrate concepts that would take many words. Don't overdo it. Use pictures for a purpose, not just to make the page look good.

Needs analysis

WBT is ideal for some sort of interactive analysis of each learner's needs. I recently designed a Web-based development need analysis tool that is used by the supervisor with the members of staff. Once the priority development needs have been properly analyzed and prioritized, the Web-based tool links into a search engine which will find suitable solutions to the needs identified.

Searchable databases

Learners can be given control over their learning by carefully indexing the learning site and giving the learner a search engine to use to find out more. In this way a lot of information can be available without appearing as hundreds of pages to be scrolled through.

Personal delivery

Personal profiles can be used to control the information any learner receives. This is quite complex at the simplest level. You can cope with different characteristics in your target group and present things in different ways. The simplest example would be different languages.

Just-in-time

WBT does not have to be done in one chunk. A Web site can be used for ongoing reference or just-in-time training, e.g., a learner may revise the key parts of 'Running meetings' just before going into a meeting.

The key point about learning objectives

Learning design for WBT is still in its infancy. One of the great dangers for learning designers is the way that learners can hop around and completely miss crucial points.

This highlights the importance of good instructional design. It is so important to break your topic down into chunks using pyramid analysis and then write a measurable objective for each chunk. This gives us clear learning markers with tests and methods of assessment that learners have to pass before they go on. How they get the knowledge and skills practice before the marker does not matter.
If there is a clear terminal objective, learners can bypass all the material, provided they can prove that they can attain the objective.

Performance support

The accessibility of Web-based learning also allows it to go beyond training into performance support. Learners can revisit WBT for just-in-time refresher training. Again, if we started our design from performance objectives first, as we recommend here, then this is no problem. What we are about is performance improvement, not training or learning. They are only the "how to's" to get somewhere else.

The distinction between training, learning, communication, and information is blurring. The important thing is performance and continuous learning, and this is why the Web is such a powerful tool:

> *It is available 365 days of the year and 24 hours a day*

> *It is real time and up to date*

> *One medium for everything:*

>> *assess your training and development needs*
>> *search for solutions*
>> *make bookings*
>> *receive training*
>> *enter discussions*
>> *do assessment — get feedback*
>> *keep your training records*

Screen design for Web-based training

Prerequisites

Screen design for Web-delivered training is fundamentally the same as for CBT and multimedia. Make sure that you read Units 1, 2, and 3 in this module before going any further.

Some general principles

Use clear, effective writing appropriate to your target group.   **see page**   177

Follow the rules for good layout.

*   choose a style and stick to it
*   avoid too much text
*   just enough white space to give an active feel
*   mix graphics and short sentences but do not overdo it
*   use unjustified right-hand margins
*   allocate areas of the screen/page for specific purposes
*   only use graphics for a purpose   **see page**   195
*   don't have lots of hyperlinks scattered through the text

Additional points for Web-based pages

*   Complex graphics will take time to load so put a simple text explanation or black-and-white drawing at the start of any complex graphic
*   Find a style sheet for text and stick to it   **see page**   196
*   Find some Web sites that you find easy to use and analyze what you think are their best features
*   Use meaningful headings and subheadings

Getting a good 'look and feel' to your pages

It is usually helpful to the user to aim for a consistent look and layout to your Web pages. This means putting your navigation controls in the same place on every page so that they are easy to find. It also means choosing a common background color to your pages. Or you can choose a background color to mark each group of pages, so that, for example, customer service modules might appear on a pale blue background while sales modules might appear on a pale pink background. Color is often a very useful visual clue as to where you are on a site if you categorize it in this way. It tells the user the moment they have stepped out of the group of pages they thought they were in.

In the words of the commercial, 'less is more.' The less cluttered your page, the more readable it is. Try to avoid lots of flashing animations and sharp, jarring colors if you want the user to read your page with any attention. Use movement initially to attract attention to a key fact on the page, but don't leave things flashing on the screen if you want the user to concentrate on any other part of the page.

The differences between screen and paper

Screens are **landscape**

Paper is **portrait**

The danger with this is that we may get long sentences presented on the screen when actually we find shorter sentences, like newspaper columns, easier to read. The way browsers and HTML work together makes this worse because the length of line on a screen can be decided by the user, not the author. Although you can control line length by putting your text into a fixed-width table. This solves the problem of very long lines on screen, but can mean that if the user is browsing through a narrow window, they will have to scroll from side to side to see a whole line of your text.

If you have a choice, splitting the screen up into columns can help readability. Otherwise, it is important to use headings and subheadings, which you have control over, to break up your material. Also remember to keep your sentences short.

Example of how the same text can look different

Warren Steel's paragraph on his Web site first looked like this;

I find the Web world to be complex and in rapid flux. I began Web authorship without much to go on, working by trial and error until I had acceptable results. Now I follow the discussions in the newsgroup comp.infosystems.www.authoring.html and try to keep up with changing standards and new browsers, while learning how best to make our documents accessible, clear, and attractive to all who browse them. To this end, I'm always making changes in my documents; in the same spirit, I'd like to offer a few suggestions in the hope that others may find 'em useful, or reply with hints of their own. This document, made in October 1995, is perpetually under revision.

Hints for Web Authors by Warren Steel

But when I looked at it through a narrow window it looked like this:

I find the Web world to be complex and in rapid flux. I began Web authorship without much to go on, working by trial and error until I had acceptable results. Now I follow the discussions in the newsgroup comp.infosystems.www.authoring.html and try to keep up with changing standards and new browsers, while learning how best to make our documents accessible, clear, and attractive to all who browse them. To this end, I'm always making changes in my documents; in the same spirit, I'd like to offer a few suggestions in the hope that others may find 'em useful, or reply with hints of their own. This document, made in October 1995, is perpetually under revision.

Hints for Web Authors by Warren Steel

A few principles for readable text on a screen

See page | 215

- *Use as little text as possible*
- *Use it big*
- *Use short lines (like newspaper columns)*
- *Present text in natural blocks, not a page at a time (Screens cost nothing, unlike paper)*
- *Do not indent*
- *Use ragged, right-hand justification which is easier to read*
- *Avoid text wrapping around graphics*
- *Edit it thoroughly*
- *Avoid using too many fonts (no more than two)*
- *Use meaningful, active headings*

Scrolling up and down

Learners will need to scroll up or down or load other pages to get the same amount of information that they would have gotten from an open book. Therefore, it is important to give consistent navigation information to let the learner know where they are just as in CBT. It is also difficult to find your way back to where you left. Bookmarking systems do help but make sure that each screen has a good identifiable title. Make your titles self explanatory, so they really tell the reader what the content is about.

Losing control over the look

Unlike a printed document, as the author you have no control over the size and typeface which the ultimate learner chooses. True, you can specify headings and sub headings so make sure these are as you want them. Remember that the browser can only display the fonts resident on the learner's PC so stick to commonplace ones.

Some key points to remember:

- *keep it simple*
- *use short sentences*
- *provide clear navigation*
- *have a clear title on each page*
- *use headings and subheadings to break up the text*

How to set up hyperlinks

Hyperlinks are one of the most powerful features of Web-based delivery, or they can be if they are done well. Hyperlinks give Web sites their informational 'power' but they can also make them utterly confusing. Here are some tips:

Keep your hyperlinks <u>short</u>

Highlight the differences in a list, not the similarities, e.g.:

- Virgin <u>Balloon Flights</u>
- Virgin <u>Atlantic Airways</u>
- Virgin <u>Radio</u>
- Virgin <u>Records</u>

Use links for a reason. Just because you can is no reason to put them in. Links should be done when the learner might want to follow up on points of specific interest which are covered in more depth elsewhere. Don't forget the option of providing links to other sites. Be aware that learners can be distracted by hyperlinks and could be in danger of hopping all over the place without learning the key principles that underline the additional detail.

Useless <u>hyperlinks</u> will catch the readers <u>eye</u> and <u>disrupt</u> the flow of information.
People also look at hyperlinks just to make sure that they are not missing anything.
You don't have to tell people to use them: "Click here to see more" is an unnecessary instruction.

Screen design cannot be done in isolation

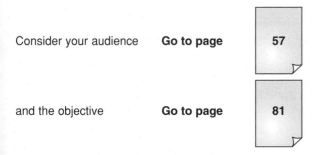

Consider your audience   **Go to page**   57

and the objective   **Go to page**   81

General principles in the use of color

Go to page   212

Keeping it strong

Roger Black, in his book, *Web Sites that Work*, suggests, "Black and white and red are the best to use, both in print and on a computer screen." You may not have any choice over the colors you use if you already have a set of standard Web sites. If you are starting from scratch make sure there are no standards that you should stick to in your organization. If there are none, then find something that you find readable from the Internet and copy the ideas.

Some examples of Web pages

Have a look at the address in the location box to find them on the Net.

Greg's Web-Based Training Place

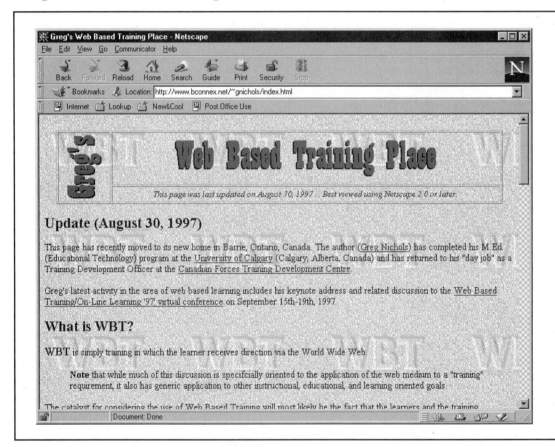

learning
points

- *too much text*
- *very wide sentences make it difficult to read*
- *paragraph breaks make it easier to read*
- *useful headings which are self-explanatory*

The Training Place

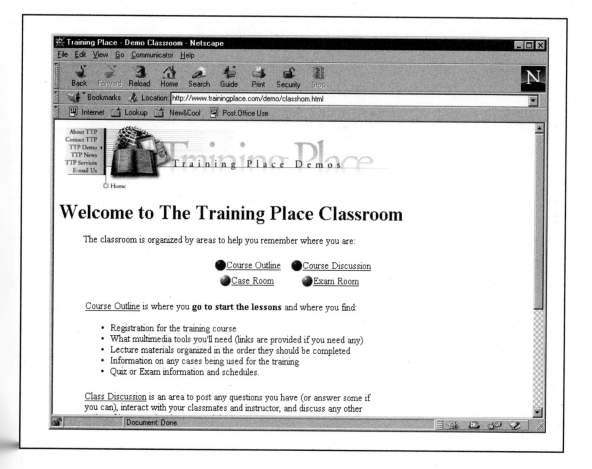

CBT Systems

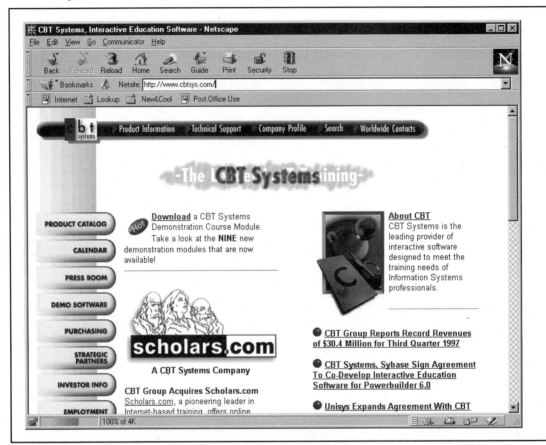

**learning
points**

- *Page split into columns like a newspaper giving short sentences which are
  easy to read*
- *plenty of hypertext links*
- *clear navigation by a consistent filing tab metaphor*
- *lines are used well to divide content*

These examples are to encourage you to have a look at some sample Web sites. Now let's see how you
would rewrite the content for WBT.

Editing exercise

Have a look at Warren Steel's two cardinal rules for Web authorship.

- take a few blank sheets of paper
- look at the examples on the previous pages
- draft out how you would present this content

---

1.   Introduction

I have two cardinal rules of Web authorship. (1) The Web is and should be platform-independent. Documents will convey the same information to users who have various operating systems (UNIX, CMS, Windows NT, Mac), various browsers (graphic, text-only, Braille, or speaking machines for the blind, etc.) and other devices (webcrawlers, searchers, indexers), and various user settings (monitor resolution, window sizes, fonts, colors, graphics turned on/off). (2) HTML is a content mark-up language, not a desktop publishing or page presentation environment. Many questions in the authoring newsgroup come from people with desktop publishing experience who want to know "how to do" something like animations, background sounds, fancy fonts and layouts, scrolling marquees, hit counters, or the like, but have no idea how to organize paragraphs, headings, lists, and images for varied platforms and displays. If you start out with good content, you can use tables, images, and other elements to enhance the appearance dramatically. If you start with a "look and feel" concept, it may be too late to pour in coherent content.

Warren Steel from his Web site

Then have a look at our version on the next page...

Editing example

1. Introduction

Two rules that you may find helpful for authoring Web sites:

- The Web is <u>platform-independent.</u>

- HTML is a <u>content mark-up language</u>
  not a desktop publishing or page presentation environment.

learning
points

- *Notice the larger font for the heading*
- *Greater use of heading and subheadings*
- *Hypertext link allows the reader to find further information if he or she wants it*
- *Changed "I" to "you"*
- *The writing from passive to active*

Editing example (continued)

1. The Web is <u>platform-independent.</u>

You can create one document to convey the same information to people using a whole range of equipment and software, including:

Operating systems:
- UNIX
- CMS
- Windows 3.x
- Windows 95
- Windows NT
- Mac OS

Browsers:
- graphic
- text-only
- Braille
- speaking machines for the blind, etc.

Devices:
- webcrawlers
- searchers
- indexers

User settings:
- monitor resolution
- window sizes
- fonts
- colors
- graphics
- turned on/off

learning points

- **You can hyperlink to a list and use the layout and headings to show the relationship between items**
- **You do not have to write in full sentences**

New things that WBT allows us to do

The Web allows us to do things that were not possible or were too expensive before. It is the ultimate multimedia delivery platform.

Web pages can be built to include pictures, text, audio, video and the text can be interactive; people can answer questions, take tests, try out procedures, ask questions, get answers, join discussion groups, and so on...

* e-mail
* on-line conferencing
* video conferencing
* CD-ROM that can be updated from the Internet

Pushed CBT

Moderated from a distance with live chat between instructors and students.

Video

Across the Internet using streaming video technology

Whiteboards

Allow people to view what is on each other's computer screens. The instructor can mark up the screen and everyone can see what they are marking up.

Real Audio

People can click on a link in a Web page and hear an audio clip. The clip can also display HTML Web pages as it plays the audio clip. Useful for telephone training or anything that involves recognizing sound (for example, teaching medical students what a heart murmur sounds like).

Virtual Reality

A virtual world is built that people can walk through and interact with. We built a successful one for training people about hazards in the office. People have to 'walk' through a virtual office and spot the potential safety hazards.

Summary

Web-based training is probably the most powerful advance in training delivery this century. It finally allows the convergence of different media onto one common platform, the desktop computer.

The principles in this guide about performance-focused training design are even more important for WBT. WBT has the potential to end the myth of the single media solution, the training video or CBT which was never a complete solution.

All learning solutions should be multimedia, using the appropriate medium for the message. All training should simulate the real performance as closely as possible. WBT for the first time gives us the tools to do the job. The only limitations are those inside the designers' heads.

Questions

---

1. What does IBT stand for?

_____ or _____ – based training

---

2. How is WBT used to manage learning?

to browse a list of _____ _____

study role-specific_____ ____

make__ ____ _____of self-directed learning materials and training

_____ learning materials

---

3. What is the most general principle for effective writing for the screen?

Use clear, effective writing_____ __ ____ _____ _____

---

4. Fill in the gaps:

- choose a ____ and stick to it
- avoid too much____
- just enough_____ _____ to give an active feel
- mix _____ and short sentences but do not overdo it
- use _____right-hand margins
- allocate areas of the screen/page for _____ _____
- only use graphics for a _____

---

5. **Who decides on the length of a line on the screen?**

6. **What does this mean to you as a designer?**

7. **Users will scroll up or down or load other pages to get the same amount of information that they would have gotten from an open book, therefore it is important that we do what, in our designs?**

8. **When setting up hyperlinks what do you do? Fill in the blanks:**

   Keep your hyperlinks _____
   Highlight the _____ in a list not the _____
   Use links for a reason.
   You don't have to ___ _____ ____ __ _____

---

9. Complete the blanks for some of the principles for readable text on a screen.

    > *Do not indent.*
    > *Use ragged, right hand justification which is easier to read.*
    > *Avoid____ _____ around graphics.*
    > *Use as little text as possible.*
    > *Edit it thoroughly.*

10. List three new things that WBL allows us to do.

11. Where would you find a beginner's guide to the Internet on the Internet?

Answers

1. What does IBT stand for?

> *Internet- or intranet-based training*

2. How is WBT used to manage learning?

> *to browse a list of <u>training solutions</u>*
> *study role-specific <u>learning maps</u>*
> *make <u>on-line booking</u> of self-directed learning materials and training*
> *<u>download</u> learning materials*

3. What is the most general principle for effective writing for the screen?

> *Use clear, effective writing <u>appropriate to your target group.</u>*

4. Fill in the gaps:

> *- choose a <u>style</u> and stick to it*
> *- avoid too much <u>text</u>*
> *- just enough <u>white space</u> to give an active feel*
> *- mix <u>graphics</u> and short sentences but do not overdo it*
> *- use <u>unjustified</u> right-hand margins*
> *- allocate areas of the screen/page for <u>specific purposes</u>*
> *- only use graphics for a <u>purpose</u>*

Answers

5. *Who decides on the length of a line on the screen?*

> *The user*

6. *What does this mean to you as a designer?*

> *It highlights the need to use headings and subheadings to break up the text.*

7. *Users will scroll up or down or load other pages to get the same amount of information that they would have gotten from an open book, therefore it is important that we do what, in our designs?*

> *Give consistent navigation information*

8. *When setting up hyperlinks what do you do? Fill in the blanks:*

> *Keep your hyperlinks <u>short.</u>*
> *Highlight the <u>differences</u> in a list, not the <u>similarities</u>.*
> *Use links for a reason.*
> *You don't have to <u>tell people to use them</u>.*

Answers

9. Complete the blanks for some of the principles for readable text on a screen.

> Do not indent.
> Use ragged, right-hand justification which is easier to read.
> Avoid text wrapping around graphics.
> Use as little text as possible.
> Edit it thoroughly.

10. List three new things that WBL allows us to do.

> on-line discussion groups
> e-mail
> on-line conferencing
> video conferencing
> CD-ROM that can be updated from the Internet
> Pushed CBT
> whiteboards
> real audio
> virtual reality

11. Where would you find a beginner's guide to the Internet on the Internet?

> **Microsoft's Internet Tutorial**　　　http://www.msn.com/tutorial/default.html

References

Anything to do with the Web is constantly changing. The best way to get up-to-date references is to look on the Web itself. Get access to the Internet and search on 'Web-based learning.' Some of the sites below may have changed by the time this book gets to print, but to get you started...

Some good sites:
The American Society for Training and Development: http://www.astd.org
Microsoft campus: http://www.microsoft.com
CBT Systems: http://www.cbtsys.com
ACT Web Site: www.actconsult.co.uk

Some more good sites:
http://www.learningconnect.com
http://www.mhonlinelearning.com
http://www.cuonline.com
http://www.open.ac.uk

For the beginner:
Microsoft's Internet Tutorial: http://www.msn.com/tutorial/default.html

For the intermediate:
How the Web Is Used Within Enterprises
http://www.cio/webmaster/sem3-intro.html
Free on-line seminar from *Webmaster* magazine.

Advanced:
Case Western University's Introduction to HTML Tutorial
http://www/cais.com/makulow/tips.html

Information:
http://www.training-info.com
Lets you search for training programs based on provider, content, location and type of delivery.

Books:
"How to Design and Post Information on a Corporate Intranet," Bryan Hopkins, Gower, 1998.
"How Internets Work," Preston Gralla, Ziff-Davis Press, 1996.
"Web Sites that Work," Roger Black, Adobe Press, 1997.

Module 4 Testing and improvement

Do your training materials keep having to be changed? This unit will show you how to plan the testing and improvement phase so that this doesn't happen.

Objective

By the end of this module you will be able to:

- *describe the main steps in the testing and improvement phase*
- *name two of the three other terms used to describe this stage*
- *state who should sign off on your draft materials before they are tested*

Testing and improvement

The next step is to test and improve our learning material. Some people call this stage *validation, product evaluation,* or *formative evaluation.*

Make sure you plan enough time for this phase

It is very important to plan enough time for this phase in the project plan. Once a manager or customer sees a lesson, he or she is in danger of thinking that it is finished and may put pressure on you to release it and start another project. However, the testing phase is critical to good self-directed learning. Unlike traditional training which can be easily modified at a later date, self-directed learning has to stand on its own.

- Don't design for nine weeks and test for one week. If it takes five weeks to produce the first draft — allow five weeks for testing and editing!

- Don't be surprised if you end up taking 30 percent of the total project time in testing and editing.

Design one module first and test with your high performer and SME and representatives from your target group to make sure that you are on the right lines. You should also show it to your customer or signatory. This could save a lot of time if it is not what they had in mind!

How to test and improve your material

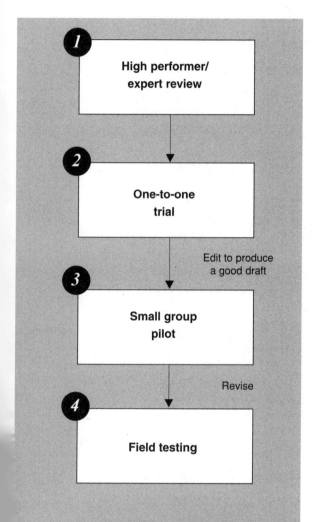

1 High performer/ expert review

2 One-to-one trial

Edit to produce a good draft

3 Small group pilot

Revise

4 Field testing

Check your rough design with your high performer.

Then check for technical accuracy with your SME.

Ask a member of the target group to try the draft material and make careful notes of what needs to be improved. You may do two or three of these.

Allow a small group of learners to use the material for real. Then collect feedback.

Answer questions:

- Can the learner achieve the objectives?
- Does he or she like the product?
- Are the test questions reliable and valid?

The four stages in more detail

1.   High performer/expert review

High performer

Check with your high performer that you have captured what he or she meant. Remember to keep things in his or her language. Write down what he or she says, not what you think you ought to write.

Subject matter expert (SME)

An expert cannot judge the effectiveness of your design; only the target group can do that. Ask him or her to check for technical accuracy, inaccuracies, or omissions.

Editorial review

It is useful at this stage for the course designer or editor to go through the entire course to identify any problems of inconsistent format, unclear directions, missing material, and poor style.

2.   One-to-one trials

These are so called because you sit with a representative sample of the target group, one-to-one, while they go through the rough draft material. Look for any hesitation, misunderstanding or difficulty with the material. Watch the learners' faces. You will need to prompt them for feedback. 'You seemed to hesitate then, why?' Students are often reluctant to comment because they think they may expose their weaknesses. You must encourage a supportive atmosphere: 'It will be the material that is wrong, not you; we will change it.'

Ironic as it may sound, it can be good to have a pair of learners as they tend to talk to each other about the lesson and you can eavesdrop.

This is the first time you will get any idea of how long your lesson may take. You will also probably get far more comments and changes than you expected. Do not be discouraged — expect them. The more changes you make to suit your target group's needs, the more successful your lessons will be!

The more one-to-one tests you can do, the better. You also need to make sure that your tests are suitable for representatives of your target group. It is no use testing your material with senior-level colleagues in the office if the target group is entry-level clerks!

3.   *Small group pilots*

These look for major problems such as omissions, inappropriate examples, inconsistencies, poor questions, and passive writing. They also validate how well students can meet the objectives. Ideally you should try to test the material on about ten members of the target group.

4.   *Field testing*

This involves large numbers of learners from the target population being tested under the actual conditions. It allows you to validate that the material really is effective for the students for whom it was designed.

Use questionnaires to collect feedback.

Collect all your comments, make further revisions, and compose the final package.

Last check

Now test the final package again and make sure you get this signed off by:

- the subject matter expert

- the customer

before you release it to the target group for full implementation.

Implementation

Even at this stage you should include feedback sheets so that students can send you their comments and suggestions. This is another phase of validation.

There is a simple example on page 304.

Example of a validation sheet

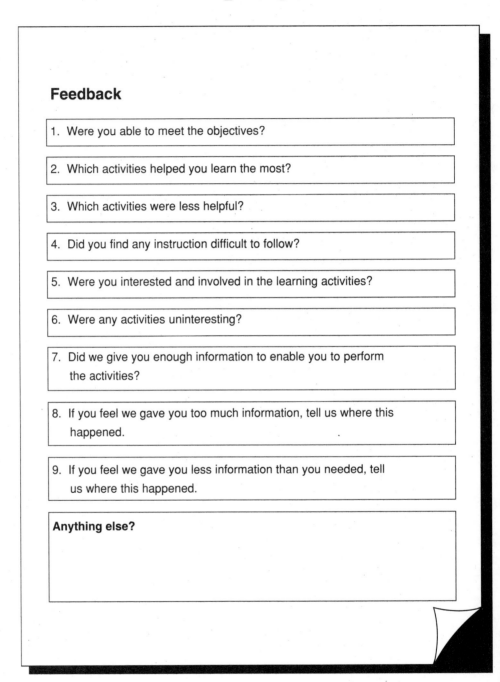

Feedback

1. Were you able to meet the objectives?

2. Which activities helped you learn the most?

3. Which activities were less helpful?

4. Did you find any instruction difficult to follow?

5. Were you interested and involved in the learning activities?

6. Were any activities uninteresting?

7. Did we give you enough information to enable you to perform the activities?

8. If you feel we gave you too much information, tell us where this happened.

9. If you feel we gave you less information than you needed, tell us where this happened.

Anything else?

Quiz

1. Describe the main steps in the testing and improvement phase.

2. Name two other terms used to describe the testing and improvement stage.

3. Who should sign off on your draft materials before they are used for testing?

4. When does validation take place?

Answers

1. Describe the main steps in the testing and improvement phase.

1.   **High performer/expert reviews**
2.   **One-to-one trials**
3.   **Small group pilots**
4.   **Field testing**

2. Name two other terms used to describe the testing and improvement stage.

- **Formative evaluation**
- **Validation**
- **Product evaluation**

3. Who should sign off on your draft materials before they are used for testing?

Subject matter expert
High performer

4. When does validation take place?

All through this phase, but particularly in small group pilots, field testing, and implementation

Module 5 Implementation

- ***Unit 1***

Implementation support

- ***Unit 2***

Project management

Unit 1

Implementation support

Have you ever wondered what happened to your training, whether you should have provided more support to aid its success? Read on...

Objective

By the end of this unit you will be able to:

- *describe the training designer's involvement in implementation*
- *state when you find out about environmental factors which might hinder implementation*

What is the designer's involvemen
in implementation?

Traditionally the customer is responsible for the successful implementation of the solutions.

However, the designer should not 'opt out' completely. He or she has a valuable role to play:

1.   In the small group pilots and field tests

To collect data about other things that are needed to ensure successful implementation, e.g., to design supporting materials for people outside the target group but who form part of the target audience, such a managers' guides, customer support materials, trainers' notes, etc.

2.   During the launch

To support the management team, possibly by explaining how the learning materials will be used.

3.   During implementation

Arrange regular reviews (say, once every four to six weeks) with your customer and users to see how the solution is going. Collect evidence of success, because successful solutions often become invisible and are not thought of as training, just 'it's the way we do things around here.'

4.   In evaluation

To make sure that the evaluation meeting you set up in the analysis phase actually takes place.

If the solutions are not proving effective, you might have to remind your customer about some of the environmental factors that you identified in the analysis. Has the incentive structure been changed? Does completion of the learning modules appear on people's performance reviews?

Quiz

1. **What is the training designer's involvement in implementation? Fill in the blanks.**

Traditionally the customer is responsible for implementation, but the training designer should:

- •

- •

- • *support the launch*

- • *design additional materials or interventions if necessary*

Answers

1. What is the training designer's involvement in implementation? Fill in the blanks.

> *Traditionally the customer is responsible for implementation, but the training designer should:*
>
> • *collect data in the small group pilots and field tests about things that might hinder implementation*
>
> • *design supporting materials for other members of the target audience, e.g., instructors' notes or managers' guides*
>
> • *support the launch*
>
> • *design additional materials or interventions if necessary*

Unit 2

Project management

Objective

By the end of this unit you will be able to:

- *describe a simple method for ensuring that every module follows the correct design process*
- *describe all the roles on a design project plan*
- *list five of the first nine steps on the design checklist for text-based material*

A project team

The stages in a systematic approach provide a very good framework to manage self-directed learning projects.

First, they allow you to identify the different roles involved and to set up a team with the required skills. A normal split for a project team would be:

•   project manager/analyst

•   designers

•   developers (programmers, desktop publishers, video specialists)

Some hints on managing projects

We will not go into project management in detail here. The skills are the same for managing any project, and if you are going to manage an self-directed learning design project you should consider getting some generic project-management training.

Some important hints:

•   Do not underestimate the time needed for testing and editing. Allow 30-50 percent of the project time for this.

•   Try and plan for slippage in the project plan and have contingency plans ready: there is always slippage.

•   Keep a frequent check on the progress against the project plan and if things are slipping take immediate action, e.g., sanction more overtime or extra resources.

There are many more, but that's the topic of another book.

A performance aid to help you manage projects

Below we have included an example of a performance aid that you might use to control your projects. We suggest you develop your own as well as page-design standards.

While you are at it, why not design a skeleton lesson showing your house style: for screen layout, use of color, etc.?

Design checklist

Package: _____   Designer: _____

High performer: _____

Module: _____   SME: _____

Stage	Name	Signature	Date
Raw material from HP Rough design complete Word-processed version Designer check High performer check SME check One-to-one test One-to-one test Design edits			
DTP Version 1			
Designer check SME check Proofreading Project manager check			
DTP Version 2			
Proofreading Small group trials Design edits			
Final DTP Version			
Gold seal Customer - Signature			
DTP Prep for printing			
Printing Distribution			

How to put together a project plan

1. List your **activities**

e.g.	a.	Research with an SME
	b.	Rough design
	c.	Typing
	d.	SME check
	e.	One-to-one trial

2. List your **tasks**

e.g.	1.	Introduction
	2.	Module 1
	3.	Module 2
	4.	Module 3
	5.	Managers' guide
	6.	Workshop

3. List your **resources**

e.g.	Designer	-	Bobby
	SME	-	Christine
	Customer	-	Brenda
	Typist	-	Dee

4. Find some **project planning sheets** with enough space for one entry per day, e.g.:

	January						
	1	2	3	4	5	6	7

Example of a project plan

On page 321 is a real example of a project plan using software called *On Target © Symantec.*

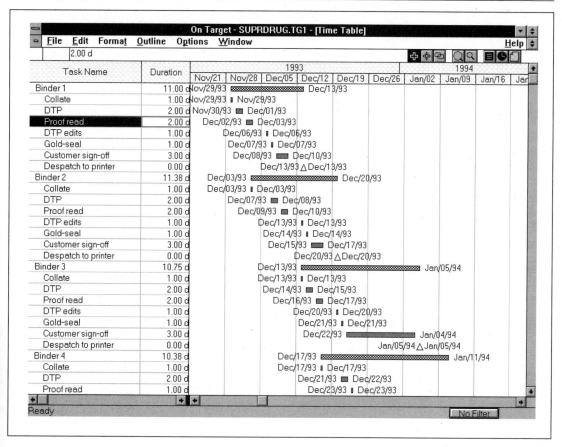

© *Symantec*

Quiz

1. **What simple method will ensure that every module follows the correct design process?**

2. **Describe all the roles on a design project plan.**

3. **Describe five of the nine steps on the design checklist that take place before desktop publishing (for text-based material).**

    -
    -
    -
    -
    -

Answers

1. **What simple method will ensure that every module follows the correct design process?**

   > *Add a design checklist to the front of each module and make sure each step is signed off.*

2. **Describe all the roles on a design project plan.**

   > - *Designer*
   > - *High performer*
   > - *Subject matter expert*
   > - *Sign off*
   > - *Project manager*

3. **Describe five of the nine steps on the design checklist that take place before desktop publishing (for text-based material).**

   > - *Raw material from high performer*
   > - *Rough design complete*
   > - *Word-processed version*
   > - *Designer check*
   > - *High performer check*
   > - *SME check*
   > - *One-to-one trial*
   > - *Design edits*
   >
   > *See design checklist on page 319.*

Module 6 Evaluation

Have you ever thought evaluation of training was difficult? This unit will explode that myth and show you how to do it.

Objective

> *By the end of this module you will be able to:*
>
> - *describe the difference between validation and evaluation*
> - *state when the key activities in evaluation take place*
> - *name those with whom you hold summative evaluation meetings*
> - *describe how you set up data collection for evaluation*
> - *describe why trainers often find evaluation difficult*
> - *describe what you evaluate in evaluation*

What is the difference between validation and evaluation?

Validation

Checking that the form of the learner's materials is valid, that they help the learner to achieve the objectives.

Evaluation

Has the desired performance been achieved? This is sometimes called **summative evaluation.**

When does validation take place?

See Module 4 because most validation takes place in:

*   small group pilots
*   field testing
*   implementation

plus interviews after implementation.

Two ways to do this are:

1. A test/quiz
2. A feedback sheet

Try the final quiz (page 339) and feedback sheet (page 304) for this book.

We are now going to validate this book.

Try the following quiz on the content. You will also find a feedback sheet on page 304.

Summative evaluation

The technical name for evaluation is summative evaluation because we look at the **summed** effects of the solutions within an organization.

Your learning package will contribute to improving someone's performance.

Evaluation begins in the analysis phase! You can only evaluate whether the target group has achieved the desired performance if this was defined in the analysis style.

The key activities in analysis are to define the measurable criterion by which you will know that the desired performance has been achieved. Think back to our DPI example. The desired performance was:

All salespeople can sell this product because they all passed the test and are licensed. Company sales targets of $2 million achieved and annual sales targets for all regions achieved for DPI.

Who do we hold evaluation meetings with?

Whoever can answer the question 'Has the desired performance been achieved?'

In our example it would probably be the sales director. It should always be your customer.

What about setting up data collection for evaluation?

This needs to be done in the analysis phase. For example, if no one knows how many salespeople are censed to sell DPI, how can we tell whether we have been successful?

Why do trainers find evaluation difficult?

1. Because they do not do a thorough enough analysis and have not set up the criterion to measure whether the desired performance has been achieved.

2. Because they try to evaluate training, which is nonsense because what we need to evaluate is performance or the ***effect*** of training on helping to improve performance.

> ### *Training is only one factor in helping to improve performance.*

> ### *You cannot evaluate training, it is only a 'how to,' not an end result.*

The evaluation of training is less important than the evaluation of the impact of training and the measurement of performance relative to delivered training.

Quiz

1. **Describe the difference between validation and evaluation.**

   Validation:

   Evaluation:

2. **State when the key activities in evaluation take place.**

3. **Name those with whom you hold summative evaluation meetings.**

4. **When do you set up data collection for evaluation?**

5. **Why do trainers often find evaluation difficult?**

6. **What should you evaluate in evaluation?**

Answers

1. Describe the difference between validation and evaluation.

> **Validation:** Checking that the form of the learning materials is valid, that they help the learner to achieve the objectives
>
> **Evaluation:** Has the desired performance been achieved? It is sometimes called summative evaluation

2. State when the key activities in evaluation take place.

> In the analysis phase

3. Name those with whom you hold summative evaluation meetings.

> Your customer

4. When do you set up data collection for evaluation?

> In the analysis phase

5. Why do trainers often find evaluation difficult?

> Because they often do not define the desired performance in the analysis phase

6. What should you evaluate in evaluation?

> Performance, not training

Summary

This book cannot cover the skill of designing effective text-based self-directed learning. It can only provide essential knowledge and some performance aids. However, these are useless until they are used. To develop skilled performance you need practice and feedback.

So you really need to work on your projects, use the book as a performance aid, and preferably get some personal coaching from a skilled designer.

Try and find someone in your organization to help. Or find out details of ACT's workshops and consultancy.

Producing an effective self-directed learning lesson involves many skills. It's a bit like watching the credits at the end of a film. Many people have been involved in a successful product.

Don't try to do it all yourself, you will fail!

Your team will take time to perfect the skills involved, but following the systematic approach in this book will help you avoid the major pitfalls and produce effective lessons.

On the next page is a summary of all the stages involved.

Good luck in your designing!

Nigel Harrison

A summary of the stages

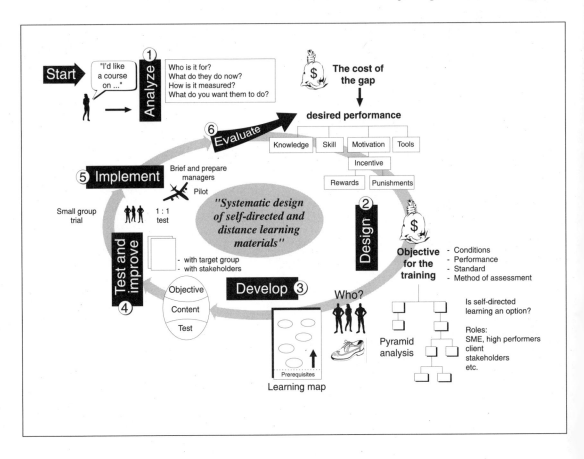

Summary

A systematic approach to designing training material

1. Analysis

- Describe the problem
- Define the problem in performance terms
- Write a measurable final objective
- Describe the target group

2. Design

- Check for other existing or possible solutions
- Use pyramid analysis to break down the objective into topics
- Write subordinate objectives
- Group sub-objectives according to learning type
- Choose media for each module
- Check the potential for using performance aids
- Write tests for each module, *then* the learning objectives

3. Development

- Produce the materials for each module

4. Testing and improvement

- One-to-one trials and small group pilots
- Revise

5. Implementation

Implement

6. Evaluation

Evaluate after a suitable period of use to see whether the desired performance has been achieved

Final quiz

Test your knowledge. Refer back to the modules if you need any help.

1. **Label the stages in the systematic approach to training design.**

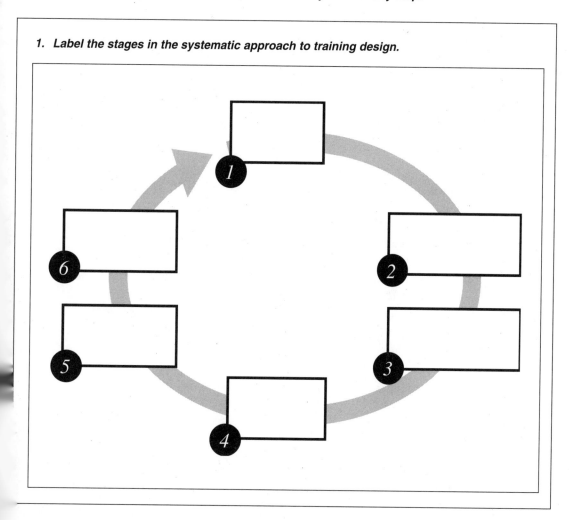

Final quiz

2. **Match each phrase with the appropriate definition below.**

1. **Analysis**

2. **Design**

3. **Development**

4. **Testing and improvement**

5. **Implementation**

6. **Summative evaluation**

a. A detailed plan of the course is produced, including the choice of media.
b. The course is used by the target audience in the intended environment.
c. The effectiveness of the course in solving the performance problem is measured.
d. Draft forms of the training material are prepared for the student trials.
e. The final objective is agreed upon and other solutions to the problem outlined.
f. Small groups of the target audience check the material for completeness and accuracy.

3. **What is the performance gap?**

The difference between

the

and

Final quiz

4. *Describe one of the first three causes of low performance.*

5. *Name three of the key factors that might justify using self-directed learning.*

1.

2.

3.

6. *What is an SME?*

7. *What is a high performer?*

Final quiz

---

8. **What is the difference between the target population and the target group?**

The target population is:

The target group is:

9. **State four elements of measurable objective.**

1.

2.

3.

4.

10. **What question do you repeatedly ask yourself when analyzing a pyramid of topics?**

11. **What are the two fundamentally different types of learning which affect how you design learning materials?**

Final quiz

12. Complete the following list of essential steps for effective instruction:

    1.   **Sell the benefits**

    2.   **Check the** _____

    3.   **Introduce - state the** _____ **objective**

    4.   **Present learning activities for the new skills or knowledge**

    5.   **Demonstrate or model the** _____ **performance and test understanding**

    6.   **Provide** _____ **and feedback**

    7.   _____ **that the performance objective can be mastered**

13. What are the following examples of?

- **a checklist**

- **a printed form**

- **a label**

14. When designing a module, after writing the objectives, what do you do next?

Final quiz

15. *What is the most important factor in selecting media?*

16. *What is the most critical thing about question design?*

17. *Rewrite the following in the active voice, personal style.*

It is important that all text appearing on the page is written with the rules for conciseness clearly in mind.

Final quiz

18. **What are the four stages of testing and improvement?**

1.

2.

3.

4.

This is the end!

How did you do?

Answers

Test your knowledge. Refer back to the modules if you need any help.

1. **Label the stages in the systematic approach to training design.**

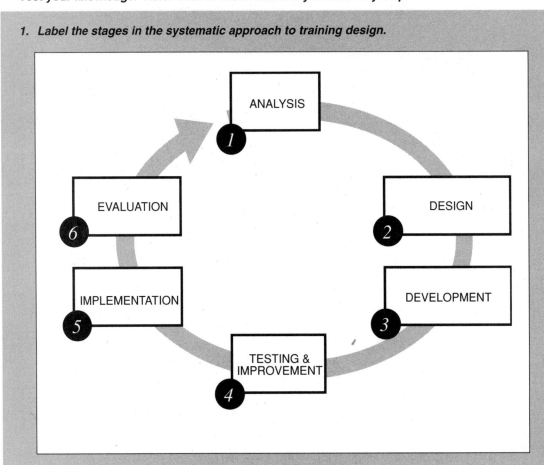

Answers

2. **Match each phrase with the appropriate definition below.**

1. Analysis | e |

2. Design | a |

3. Development | d |

4. Testing and improvement | f |

5. Implementation | b |

6. Summative evaluation | c |

a. A detailed plan of the course is produced, including the choice of media.
b. The course is used by the target audience in the intended environment.
c. The effectiveness of the course in solving the performance problem is measured.
d. Draft forms of the training material are prepared for the student trials.
e. The final objective is agreed upon and other solutions to the problem outlined.
f. Small groups of the target audience check the material for completeness and accuracy.

3. **What is the performance gap?**

The difference between

the | desired performance |

and | actual performance |

Answers

4. **Describe one of the first three causes of low performance.**

1. Poor information/unclear expectations	4. Lack of knowledge
2. Difficult environment/inadequate equipment	5. Lack of skills
3. Poor incentives	6. Poor motivation

5. **Name three of the key factors that might justify using self-directed learning.**

1. *A large target group*

2. *Geographically dispersed*

3. *The training needs to be repeated often*

4. *The material has a long shelf-life*

5. *People want to enter training with variable levels of skill and knowledge*

6. *People need to learn at their own pace, place, and time*

6. **What is an SME?**

Subject matter expert

7. **What is a high performer?**

Somebody who already does the job well

8. **What is the difference between the target population and the target group?**

    The target population is:

    > **All the people who may use the course**

    The target group is:

    > **The main users of the course**

9. **State four elements of measurable objective.**

    1. **Conditions**

    2. **Performance**

    3. **Standard**

    4. **Method of assessment**

10. **What question do you repeatedly ask yourself when analyzing a pyramid of topics?**

    > **What does the person need to be able to do in order to perform at this higher level?**

11. **What are the two fundamentally different types of learning which affect how you design learning materials?**

    - **Knowledge**

    - **Skills**

Answers

12. Complete the following list of essential steps for effective instruction:

1. **Sell the benefits**

2. **Check the** | **prerequisites** |

3. **Introduce — state the** | **performance** | **objective**

4. **Present learning activities for the new skills or knowledge**

5. **Demonstrate or model the** | **desired** | **performance and test understanding**

6. **Provide** | **practice** | **and feedback**

7. | **Test** | **that the performance objective can be mastered**

13. What are the following examples of?

- a checklist

- a printed form   **Performance aids**

- a label

14. When designing a module, after writing the objectives, what do you do next?

Design the test

Answers

15. *What is the most important factor in selecting media?*

> That it is as close to the real performance as possible

16. *What is the most critical thing about question design?*

> That questions come directly from the performance objective and are relevant tests of the desired performance

17. *Rewrite the following in the active voice, personal style.*

It is important that all text appearing on the page is written with the rules for conciseness clearly in mind.

> Write it concisely

Answers

18. *What are the four stages of testing and improvement?*

1. *Expert/high performer review*

2. *One-to-one trials*

3. *Small group pilots*

4. *Field testing*

Bibliography

This book is a collection of applied theory from numerous sources over the years. I have been influenced by many designers and helped by suggestions from countless students on my workshops.

Anderson Seiler, B., *Guidelines for Designing PLATO Lessons.* University of Delaware, 1981.

Avner, R.A. 'How to produce ineffective CAL material,' *Educational Technology*, August 1971.

Beech, G., *Computer Based Learning.* Sigma Technical Press, 1983.

Boydell, T.H., *A Guide to Job Analysis*. Bacie, 1973.

Boydell, T.H., *A Guide to the Identification of Training Needs*. Bacie, 1973.

Carter, R., *Systems Management and Change*, P.C.P. Paul Chapman Ltd. in association with The Open University.

Control Data Corporation, *Courseware Development Process*, 1979.

Dean, C. and Whitlock, Q., *A Handbook of Computer-Based Training*, 2nd edition. Kogan Page, 1988.

Fletcher, Shirley, *Designing Competence-Based Training.* Kogan Page, 1991.

Heines, J., 'Writing objectives with style,' *Training*, December 1979.

Heines, J.M., *Screen Design Strategies for Computer-Assisted Instruction.* Digital Press, 1984.

Heines, J., 'Anybody can't do CBT. A team approach to course development,' *Training News*, March 1985.

Heines, J., 'Interactive means active, learner involvement in CBT data,' *Training*, March 1985.

Hottos, S., *CD-I Designers Guide.* McGraw-Hill, 1993.

Mager, R.F., *Preparing Instructional Objectives.* David S. Lake Publishers, 1984.

Mager, R.F. and Beech, G., *Developing Vocational Instruction*, 1st edition. Fearon Publishers, 1967.

Mager, R.F. and Pipe, P., *Analysing Performance Problems.* David S. Lake Publishers, 1970.

Mager, R.F. and Pipe, P., *Performance Analysis Flowchart*. David S. Lake Publishers, 1979.

Mager, R.F. and Pipe, P., *Performance Analysis Worksheet.* David S. Lake Publishers, 1979.

Romiszowski, A. J., *Designing Instructional Systems.* Kogan Page, 1981.

Romiszowski, A. J., *Developing Auto-Instructional Materials.* Kogan Page, 1986.

THE END

Credits

With thanks to Paul for his brilliant page design Christian for his desktop publishing, Michael Molinaro for his careful editing and ideas and Jenny for her help with the Web-based training unit.

Nigel Harrison

Index

Index

E

F

G

H

I

J

K

L

M

O

P

Q

R

S

T

U

V

W